Future Fear Future Faith

Future Fear Future Faith

Jacob Nand

Published by Howard Hirsch Publishing, 2025.

FUTURE FEAR FUTURE FAITH

First edition. January 27, 2025.

ISBN: 979-8230394013

Written by Jacob Nand.

Table of Contents

Forward: Why Are We Afraid?

Americans are currently navigating a particularly tense and uncertain political climate, driven by both domestic and global events that have raised concerns about the future. From increasing polarization at home to growing geopolitical tensions abroad, many Americans are experiencing a sense of nervousness and apprehension. This anxiety is not only shaped by immediate concerns but also by deep-seated fears about the stability and direction of the country. To understand why so many are nervous, it is necessary to explore the current political landscape, the state of international relations, and the underlying factors contributing to this unease.

1. Political Polarization

One of the most significant reasons for nervousness in the United States is the deepening political polarization that has taken hold in recent years. In many ways, the political divide between the two major parties, Republicans and Democrats, has never been more pronounced. In the past, American politics often had room for bipartisan collaboration and compromise, but today, there seems to be an increasing inability to find common ground. The ideological gap between the parties has grown, with many Americans feeling more aligned with their respective party's positions than ever before.

This polarization is not only reflected in the policies and rhetoric of political leaders but also in the way Americans interact with one another. Voters now tend to surround themselves with like-minded individuals, reinforcing their views through echo chambers in social media and media outlets. This deep divide is reflected in both the political discourse and the emotional intensity of debates. Issues such as healthcare, gun rights, climate change, and immigration have become highly contentious, with little room for compromise.

The consequence of this polarization is that many Americans feel disillusioned and increasingly alienated from the political system.

People are frustrated that politicians seem more interested in advancing party lines than in addressing the needs and concerns of the public. This frustration can turn into fear about the future of democracy itself. Many Americans fear that the country is headed towards an era of political gridlock, where meaningful change becomes impossible, and that the institutions designed to protect democracy could become weakened or compromised.

2. The 2024 Election and Uncertainty about Leadership

Americans are nervous about the legitimacy of the 2024 election. The previous election, in 2020, left the country deeply divided, and the aftermath of the events surrounding the storming of the Capitol on January 6, 2021, only further polarized the nation. Many Americans are anxious about the stability of the electoral process and whether the results of future elections will be the actual will of the voters and will be accepted by all parties involved.

A major concern is the continuation of Donald Trump's influence on American politics. Despite losing the 2020 election, Trump remained a dominant force in the Republican Party, with many of his supporters believing that the 2020 election was "stolen." His rhetoric has continued to fuel the belief that the U.S. government is corrupt and that election results cannot be trusted.

Trump's apparent success, marred by irregularities in the 2024 election has many Americans fearful that he could escalate tensions and further undermine trust in the democratic process.

Americans question whether Biden, at 82 years old, would be able to successfully carry out another presidential campaign and, if re-elected, complete a second term due to his performance on one night. A disastrous showing in a presidential debate. Some argue that his age was a liability, particularly as he faced mounting criticism over the state of the economy and his handling of foreign policy.

Mainstream media seized on the performance as a way to drum up interest in their publications and keep their readers' interest.

This uncertainty around the leadership of both major parties contributes to a sense of nervousness. Americans were left wondering who would lead the country in the next election and whether they will be able to restore unity and tackle the pressing issues facing the nation.

3. The State of the Economy

Economic instability is another key factor driving anxiety among Americans. While the U.S. economy experienced significant growth following the initial waves of the COVID-19 pandemic, the recovery has been uneven, and many Americans continue to struggle with rising living costs, particularly in the areas of housing, healthcare, and education. Inflation has been a central issue, with the prices of everyday goods and services rising rapidly. This has eroded the purchasing power of middle-class families, who feel that they are not receiving adequate support from the government or from businesses.

The job market, while strong in 2024, remains precarious for many workers. The rise of automation, the gig economy, and the shifting landscape of work due to the pandemic have left many Americans uncertain about job security. There is also a growing concern about the sustainability of Social Security and other entitlement programs that millions of Americans rely on for their retirement and healthcare needs.

Additionally, concerns about the national debt and the government's fiscal health are increasing. Many Americans worry that the country's growing debt will eventually lead to higher taxes, inflation, or cuts to important social programs. These economic fears are exacerbated by the political gridlock in Washington, where Congress seems unable to pass meaningful legislation to address these issues.

4. The Rise of Extremist Movements

Another source of anxiety in the U.S. is the rise of extremist political movements on both the far-left and far-right. These groups, which are increasingly active and vocal, pose a threat to the social fabric of the country and to the stability of democratic institutions. On the far-right, white nationalist and militia groups have gained prominence, advocating for a more authoritarian approach to governance and a rejection of the multicultural ideals that have long been central to American identity. On the far-left, radical activists have pushed for sweeping changes to the political system, including defunding the police and dismantling capitalist institutions.

The actions and rhetoric of these extremist groups have created a sense of fear and uncertainty among many Americans. In particular, the January 6 Capitol riot, which was fueled by far-right extremists, has left lasting scars on the national consciousness. The images of rioters storming the U.S. Capitol in an attempt to overturn a legitimate election result have reinforced fears of political violence and civil unrest.

At the same time, the increase in violent protests and the growing power of radical right wing movements such a the MAGA (Make America Great Again) movement and left-wing movements, such as those associated with BLM, (Black Lives Matter) has also contributed to a sense of insecurity. These movements, while largely peaceful, have sometimes been associated with property damage and confrontations with law enforcement, further fueling fears about social instability. The January 6, 2021 insurrection on the US Capitol instilled fear in people of all parties and the pardon of the violent insurrectionists added a new level of perceived danger.

The rise of these extremist factions has led to a sense of vulnerability among many Americans, who fear that the country is becoming more divided and that radical elements will push the nation toward more violent and disruptive political outcomes.

5. Global Instability and Geopolitical Tensions

Beyond domestic concerns, Americans are also anxious about the state of the world and the potential for global conflicts. The geopolitical landscape has become increasingly volatile in recent years, with tensions rising between major powers like the U.S., China, and Russia. The war in Ukraine has been a particular point of concern, as it has not only resulted in widespread human suffering but also raised the specter of broader military conflict, including the possibility of direct confrontation between NATO and Russia.

In addition to the conflict in Ukraine, the U.S. is facing growing tensions with China, particularly over issues related to Taiwan, trade, and human rights. Many Americans are worried about the economic and military implications of these tensions, as China is both a critical global trading partner and a potential adversary. The growing influence of China on the global stage has created anxiety about the future of American global dominance and the potential for a new Cold War.

The threat of terrorism and the rise of authoritarianism in other parts of the world, such as in Iran and North Korea, add to the sense of global instability. The United States has long been the leader of the free world, but as global power dynamics shift, many Americans are uncertain about the country's role in an increasingly multipolar world. The fear of being dragged into a major international conflict, whether in Europe, Asia, or the Middle East, contributes to the broader sense of unease.

6. Climate Change and Environmental Crisis

In addition to political and economic concerns, many Americans are deeply worried about the growing environmental crisis and the existential threat posed by climate change. The increasing frequency of extreme weather events, such as hurricanes, wildfires, and droughts, has made the effects of climate change more visible and urgent. Many

Americans are anxious about the long-term impact of these changes, particularly on future generations.

There is also concern about the government's response to climate change. While some politicians and policymakers are pushing for bold action to address the crisis, others continue to downplay the severity of the issue or oppose measures to reduce carbon emissions. This divide has led to frustration among environmental advocates, who feel that the political system is not taking the crisis seriously enough.

Furthermore, the environmental toll of economic development and the extraction of natural resources has raised concerns about the sustainability of the country's way of life. Issues such as pollution, deforestation, and the loss of biodiversity are contributing to a broader sense of environmental anxiety. Many Americans fear that the country's failure to act decisively on climate change could lead to irreversible damage to the planet.

7. The Impact of Technology and Social Media

The role of technology and social media in shaping public opinion and political discourse is another factor contributing to nervousness in the United States. The rise of digital platforms has transformed the way people communicate and engage with political issues, but it has also created new challenges. The spread of misinformation, the manipulation of public opinion through targeted ads, and the increasing fragmentation of the media landscape have made it more difficult for Americans to distinguish fact from fiction.

Social media platforms, such as Twitter, Facebook, and Instagram, have become key arenas for political debate and activism, but they have also amplified extremism, conspiracy theories, and hate speech. The algorithm-driven nature of these platforms often reinforces users' existing beliefs, contributing to the fragmentation of the public sphere and the erosion of trust in traditional news outlets. This environment has left many Americans feeling overwhelmed and confused, unsure of where to turn for accurate information.

The rise of artificial intelligence and surveillance technologies has also raised concerns about privacy and personal freedom. Many Americans worry about the increasing role of technology in everyday life, particularly in relation to government surveillance and the potential for authoritarian control. The balance between national security and individual freedoms is a delicate one, and many Americans are nervous about the growing power of tech companies and government agencies to monitor and control their lives.

Where We Stand

The current political and global landscape has created a perfect storm of anxiety for many Americans. Domestic issues such as political polarization, economic instability, and the rise of extremist movements are compounded by global challenges like geopolitical tensions, climate change, and the impact of technology. Concerns about leadership and the future direction of the country are only intensifying. As Americans face these challenges, they are left wondering whether their country can overcome its divisions and find a path toward stability and unity. The nervousness that permeates the national consciousness is not just a reaction to current events but also a reflection of deeper fears about the future of democracy, the economy, and the environment.

The Before Times

Before the election of Donald Trump in 2016, America was grappling with a variety of political, economic, and societal challenges that would shape the landscape of the 21st century. The period leading up to the first election of Donald Trump marked a time of intense political polarization, a slowly recovering economy after the 2008 financial crisis, and a rapidly changing demographic and social landscape. In many ways, the election of Donald Trump transformed key issues such as economic recovery, political polarization, demographic shifts, social issues, foreign policy, and the changing nature of American political identity.

The Economic Landscape: Post-Recession Recovery

The most significant economic event of the early 21st century was the global financial crisis of 2008. Triggered by the collapse of major financial institutions, the subsequent recession resulted in a sharp contraction of the U.S. economy, massive job losses, and a steep decline in household wealth. The recovery from this crisis was slow and uneven, leaving many Americans disillusioned with the political establishment and searching for new leadership that could address their frustrations.

By the time of the 2016 election, the U.S. economy had technically emerged from the recession. The stock market had rebounded, and the unemployment rate had fallen, but economic recovery had been uneven, particularly in industrial areas and among lower-income Americans. The recovery primarily benefited the wealthiest Americans and large corporations, while many working-class and middle-class families continued to struggle with stagnant wages, rising healthcare costs, and job insecurity. Additionally, many of the manufacturing jobs that had once been the backbone of the American economy had been lost to outsourcing and automation.

During President Barack Obama's second term, the economy had grown steadily, but for many Americans, it felt as though the recovery was not trickling down to them. The growing gap between the rich and the poor, combined with the loss of traditional blue-collar jobs, created a sense of economic anxiety. In 2016, this frustration reached a boiling point. Many Americans, particularly in the Rust Belt, felt that the political establishment had ignored their struggles and failed to address the structural problems in the economy. This resentment would later fuel the rise of Donald Trump, who promised to "Make America Great Again" by bringing back jobs and reversing the economic decline in certain regions.

Political Polarization and the Decline of Bipartisanship

By the time of Trump's first election, political polarization in the U.S. had reached new heights. The period leading up to 2016 saw an increasing divide between the two major political parties, with little room for bipartisan cooperation. This polarization was driven by ideological differences, but also by an increasingly partisan media landscape that further entrenched Americans' political views.

The rise of the Tea Party movement in the early 2010s, a conservative response to the Obama administration's policies, signaled the growing divide between liberals and conservatives. The movement was particularly influential in the Republican Party, pushing the party further to the right and encouraging a combative stance toward government spending, healthcare reform, and social policies. The Democrats, on the other hand, had been significantly reshaped by the election of Barack Obama in 2008, which solidified their role as the party of diversity, social justice, and progressive policies on issues like healthcare, climate change, and immigration.

The period leading up to the 2016 election was also marked by the rise of extreme partisan rhetoric, with political figures frequently attacking each other's motives and accusing their opponents of undermining American values. This environment made it increasingly difficult for politicians to work together on key issues. The country was also deeply divided over issues like Obamacare (the Affordable Care Act), with Republicans vowing to repeal it and Democrats defending it as a major accomplishment of the Obama presidency. The two-party system had become so polarized that even basic legislative processes, such as passing a budget or confirming judicial appointments, were often met with gridlock and partisan obstruction.

This political environment contributed to the sense of frustration that many Americans felt with their elected representatives. Many voters felt that their voices were not being heard and that the political elite, regardless of party affiliation, were out of touch with the needs of ordinary Americans. The rise of Donald Trump as a political outsider was a direct response to this disillusionment, as he campaigned on the idea of breaking away from the political establishment and delivering a more populist, unfiltered approach to leadership.

Demographic Changes and Identity Politics

One of the most significant societal shifts in the years leading up to the 2016 election was the changing demographic landscape of the United States. Immigration, both legal and illegal, had become a central issue in American politics, particularly with the increasing number of Latino, Asian, and Middle Eastern immigrants arriving in the U.S. These demographic shifts were changing the character of American society and, by extension, American politics.

As the U.S. became more racially and ethnically diverse, identity politics began to play a more prominent role in national conversations. Issues such as racial inequality, police brutality, and immigration reform were at the forefront of public discourse. The Black Lives

Matter movement, which began in 2013 in response to the shooting of Trayvon Martin and the acquittal of George Zimmerman, became a major force in shaping discussions about race and policing in America. Similarly, the debate over immigration reform reached a fever pitch, with the Obama administration attempting to implement executive actions like DACA (Deferred Action for Childhood Arrivals) to protect undocumented immigrants brought to the U.S. as children.

For many white Americans, particularly those without college degrees, these demographic changes were a source of anxiety. As the country became more diverse, many felt that their cultural and political influence was waning. This sense of cultural displacement was particularly acute in rural and working-class communities that had been hit hardest by economic globalization and the decline of traditional industries. Donald Trump tapped into these fears by positioning himself as a defender of traditional American values, promising to limit immigration and protect American jobs from foreign competition.

At the same time, the rise of social movements advocating for the rights of women, LGBTQ+ individuals, and racial minorities further contributed to a growing sense of division. Issues like same-sex marriage, transgender rights, and reproductive rights were central to the progressive agenda, but they also generated intense backlash from conservative and religious communities. The increasing visibility of these social justice movements in American life highlighted the cultural and political divides between urban and rural areas, and between more liberal and more conservative parts of the country.

Social and Cultural Issues: The Erosion of Trust

In the years leading up to the 2016 election, Americans were also grappling with a crisis of trust in their institutions. Scandals, corruption, and failures in governance had eroded the public's faith in the political system. The most significant scandal of the early 21st century was the Iraq War, which many Americans felt was based on false pretenses. The weapons of mass destruction (WMDs) that were cited as justification for the invasion never materialized, leading to widespread distrust of the government, particularly among liberals who had opposed the war from the beginning.

In addition to foreign policy failures, domestic issues also contributed to the erosion of trust in institutions. The 2008 financial crisis, which exposed deep flaws in the banking and financial systems, left many Americans disillusioned with the notion of American exceptionalism and the belief that the U.S. was a land of opportunity for all. The bailout of major financial institutions, which was seen by many as an example of "crony capitalism," fueled anger and resentment toward Wall Street and the political elite who had protected it.

These societal and cultural divisions were further amplified by the growing role of social media in shaping political discourse. The rise of platforms like Facebook, Twitter, and YouTube transformed the way Americans interacted with politics, enabling individuals to engage with like-minded communities and reinforcing ideological echo chambers. This shift created an environment in which facts and truth became increasingly contested, with misinformation and fake news playing a significant role in shaping public opinion.

For many Americans, the 2016 election was not just a referendum on the political and economic conditions of the country but also a moment of reckoning with the deep divisions within society. Donald Trump's campaign, with its focus on "draining the swamp" and attacking the media, was seen by many as a response to this distrust of traditional institutions and political elites.

Foreign Policy and America's Role in the World

The U.S. role in global affairs was another central issue leading up to the 2016 election. The aftermath of the Iraq War, the rise of terrorism, and the ongoing conflicts in the Middle East were all major challenges for the Obama administration. The Obama administration had pursued a policy of multilateralism, seeking to strengthen alliances and engage in diplomacy, but this approach was met with mixed results. The rise of ISIS and the instability in Libya and Syria were seen by many as failures of Obama's foreign policy.

At the same time, the U.S. was increasingly engaged with rising powers like China and Russia, and many Americans were concerned about the shifting balance of power in global politics. Issues such as trade, national security, and military presence abroad were central to the debate over the U.S.'s role in the world. Donald Trump's "America First" campaign promised to prioritize American interests and reduce the U.S.'s involvement in global conflicts, a stance that resonated with voters who were disillusioned with the foreign policy establishment and skeptical of the country's continued military presence in the Middle East.

Trump's populist rhetoric and calls for protectionism and nationalism were appealing to many voters who felt that globalization had led to job losses, stagnant wages, and a decline in American manufacturing. His stance on trade, particularly his promises to renegotiate NAFTA and impose tariffs on China, was seen as a way to protect American workers and restore the country's economic standing in the world.

Anger Votes

The political and societal conditions of America before the first election of Donald Trump were marked by deep divisions, economic uncertainty, and a growing sense of distrust in institutions. The aftermath of the 2008 financial crisis, the rise of partisan polarization, the changing demographic landscape, and the erosion of trust in government all contributed to a climate of frustration and disillusionment. The election of Donald Trump in 2016 was, in many ways, a response to these challenges, as Trump tapped into the anger and anxieties of voters who felt left behind by the political establishment. His victory marked a turning point in American politics, ushering in a new era of populism, nationalism, and political upheaval that would continue to shape the country in the years to come.

The First Trump Administration

The first Trump administration, which lasted from January 2017 to January 2021, had a profound and multifaceted impact on Americans. Donald Trump's presidency was marked by a series of controversial policies, divisive rhetoric, and a starkly different approach to governance than previous administrations. His time in office left an indelible mark on American politics, society, and culture. To understand the full effect of the first Trump administration on Americans, it is crucial to examine the major areas of impact, including political polarization, the economy, social issues, foreign policy, and public health. Additionally, the long-term consequences of his leadership, both positive and negative, shaped the trajectory of the country and its citizens.

1. Political Polarization and Divisiveness

One of the most significant and lasting effects of Donald Trump's first term was the deepening of political polarization in the United States. Prior to his election, American politics had already been experiencing growing ideological divides, but Trump's presidency took these divisions to new extremes. His rhetoric and policies often served to inflame tensions between conservative and liberal factions, further separating the country along political lines.

Trump's leadership style, characterized by his frequent use of inflammatory language and combative rhetoric, helped to galvanize both his supporters and his detractors. He regularly used social media, particularly Twitter, to communicate directly with the American public, bypassing traditional media channels and fueling a highly partisan narrative. This created a stark contrast between his supporters, who saw him as a champion of the working class and an outsider fighting the "deep state," and his critics, who viewed him as a dangerous demagogue undermining democratic institutions and norms.

The administration's approach to governance often involved a stark "us vs. them" mentality. Trump frequently attacked political opponents, the media, and various groups that he viewed as enemies of his agenda. The partisan rancor reached new heights, with Congress frequently gridlocked, particularly after Democrats took control of the House of Representatives in 2019. The bitter political battles, which included high-profile impeachment proceedings and ongoing investigations into the administration's actions, contributed to an environment where cooperation across party lines became increasingly rare.

The polarization of American society also manifested in public protests and demonstrations. The rise of the Black Lives Matter movement, which gained renewed attention after the 2016 election, culminated in widespread protests following the killing of George Floyd by a police officer in 2020. Trump's handling of these protests, which included calling for the use of military force against demonstrators and his refusal to engage with calls for police reform, only deepened divisions between supporters of racial justice and those who felt his rhetoric was a defense of law and order.

2. Economic Impact: Job Growth, Tax Cuts, and Trade Wars

When Donald Trump took office, one of his main promises was to revitalize the American economy. His administration focused on tax cuts, deregulation, and boosting domestic manufacturing. Early in his presidency, the U.S. economy continued to recover from the Great Recession, which had occurred under the previous administration, and Trump capitalized on this recovery.

Tax Reform and Economic Growth

The most significant economic policy enacted by Trump was the Tax Cuts and Jobs Act of 2017. This legislation lowered the corporate tax rate from 35% to 21% and provided temporary tax cuts for individuals. Proponents of the tax cuts argued that they would stimulate economic growth by encouraging businesses to invest and hire more workers. Indeed, the tax cuts were associated with an increase in corporate profits and a stock market boom, with the S&P 500 reaching record highs in 2017 and 2018.

However, critics of the tax cuts argued that they disproportionately benefited the wealthy and large corporations while doing little for middle- and working-class Americans. While the tax cuts were expected to pay for themselves through increased economic growth, the national deficit rose significantly during Trump's first term, as tax revenues failed to keep pace with government spending. By the end of his presidency, the U.S. had accumulated a record national debt, which raised concerns about the long-term sustainability of these policies.

Job Growth and Economic Disparities

During the early years of the Trump administration, the U.S. economy saw a steady increase in job growth, with unemployment reaching record lows before the onset of the COVID-19 pandemic. The stock market also performed well, and many Americans benefited from rising asset values, including home prices. However, the benefits of economic growth were unevenly distributed. While some sectors, such as technology and finance, thrived, others, particularly in manufacturing, were left behind.

Trump's trade policies, especially his tariffs on Chinese goods, aimed to protect American jobs and industries that were seen as vulnerable to foreign competition. While some industries, such as steel and aluminum, saw short-term benefits from these tariffs, the broader impact was mixed. Tariffs increased the cost of goods for consumers, and the trade war with China led to significant disruptions in global supply chains. Farmers, in particular, were adversely affected by retaliatory tariffs, leading to a decline in exports and financial hardship for many agricultural communities.

The COVID-19 Pandemic and Economic Recession

The COVID-19 pandemic had a profound effect on the U.S. economy, leading to widespread job losses, business closures, and a sharp contraction in economic activity. The Trump administration's handling of the pandemic became one of the most controversial aspects of his presidency. While Trump initially downplayed the severity of the virus, calling it a "hoax" and suggesting it would soon disappear, his administration eventually implemented policies like the Paycheck Protection Program (PPP) to provide financial assistance to businesses and individuals.

Despite these efforts, millions of Americans lost their jobs, and the economic recession caused by the pandemic plunged the country into a crisis. By the end of 2020, the unemployment rate had spiked to nearly 15%, and many Americans faced uncertainty about their economic futures. The pandemic also highlighted the deep inequalities in American society, with marginalized communities disproportionately affected by the virus and its economic fallout.

3. Social Issues: Immigration, Healthcare, and Civil Rights

The Trump administration's impact on social issues was one of the most divisive aspects of his presidency. His policies on immigration, healthcare, and civil rights were often controversial, sparking fierce debates across the country.

Immigration and Border Security

One of Trump's signature campaign promises was to build a wall along the southern border with Mexico to prevent illegal immigration. Throughout his presidency, he focused on restricting immigration and cracking down on undocumented migrants. His administration implemented a "zero tolerance" policy that led to the separation of thousands of children from their parents at the U.S.-Mexico border. This policy was widely condemned, and many Americans viewed it as a violation of human rights. While the Trump administration defended its actions as necessary for border security, the policy fueled a national conversation about immigration and the treatment of migrant families.

Trump also sought to end programs like DACA (Deferred Action for Childhood Arrivals), which provided protections for undocumented immigrants brought to the U.S. as children. The administration's attempts to rescind DACA were met with legal challenges, and the issue remained unresolved for much of his presidency.

Healthcare: Repeal and Replace

Another major issue during Trump's first term was the repeal of the Affordable Care Act (ACA), also known as Obamacare. Trump and many Republicans viewed the ACA as an overreach of government power and sought to dismantle it. However, despite multiple attempts to repeal the ACA, Trump was unable to fulfill this promise fully. The Republican-controlled Senate failed to pass a comprehensive repeal, and the most significant change was the elimination of the individual mandate, which required Americans to have health insurance or face a penalty.

Despite this setback, Trump's administration did succeed in pushing for policies that made healthcare less accessible for some Americans. For example, the administration expanded the availability of short-term, limited-duration health plans that did not have to comply with ACA regulations. These plans were often cheaper but offered less coverage, leaving many Americans vulnerable to high medical costs.

Civil Rights and Racial Tensions

Trump's presidency was also marked by an intensification of racial tensions in the United States. His handling of incidents of racial violence, particularly the white nationalist rally in Charlottesville in 2017, drew sharp criticism. Trump's response, which included claiming there were "very fine people on both sides," was widely condemned as a failure to denounce white supremacy. His rhetoric on issues of race, including his attacks on NFL players who protested racial injustice by kneeling during the national anthem, contributed to a sense that the president was hostile to the concerns of African Americans and other minority communities.

The Trump administration also took steps to roll back civil rights protections in areas such as housing and education. For example, the Department of Education under Trump moved to reduce the enforcement of policies designed to combat discrimination in schools, including Title IX protections for transgender students. These moves were viewed by many as a step backward for civil rights and social justice.

4. Foreign Policy: America First and Global Relations

Trump's foreign policy, encapsulated in his "America First" slogan, represented a significant departure from traditional U.S. diplomacy. His approach emphasized national sovereignty, skepticism toward international alliances, and a desire to reduce the U.S. role in global affairs.

Trade Policy and Tariffs

Trump's administration took a confrontational approach to trade, particularly with China. He imposed tariffs on hundreds of billions of dollars' worth of Chinese goods, claiming that China had engaged in unfair trade practices and intellectual property theft. While these tariffs were intended to address trade imbalances and protect American workers, they also disrupted global supply chains and hurt many industries. Trump's trade war with China, while garnering support from some sectors, ultimately proved to be a double-edged sword.

Relationship with Allies

Trump's "America First" stance strained U.S. relationships with many of its traditional allies. He frequently criticized NATO and other international organizations, questioning their value and whether other countries were contributing enough to collective defense. Trump's unorthodox approach to diplomacy extended to his relationship with North Korea's Kim Jong-un, whom he met with several times in an attempt to negotiate denuclearization. While Trump's outreach to North Korea was seen as a bold move, critics argued that it lacked tangible results and may have legitimized an authoritarian regime.

The Middle East

Trump's foreign policy in the Middle East was marked by significant shifts. His administration pulled the U.S. out of the Iran nuclear deal, which had been negotiated under the Obama administration, and imposed harsh sanctions on Iran. This move heightened tensions in the region and led to military confrontations between the U.S. and Iran.

In contrast, Trump's approach to Israel was one of the most visible aspects of his Middle East policy. His administration recognized Jerusalem as the capital of Israel and moved the U.S. embassy there, a move that was controversial and seen as a departure from longstanding U.S. policy. However, his administration also brokered a series of normalization agreements between Israel and several Arab nations, known as the Abraham Accords, which were viewed as a significant diplomatic achievement.

5. Public Health: The COVID-19 Pandemic

The COVID-19 pandemic, which emerged in early 2020, had a devastating impact on Americans, both in terms of public health and the economy. Trump's handling of the crisis was widely criticized, particularly for downplaying the severity of the virus in its early stages and for inconsistent messaging from public health experts. The administration's response to the pandemic was marked by confusion and missteps, including delays in testing, shortages of personal protective equipment, and a lack of coordinated federal action.

As the virus spread across the country, Trump's messaging remained inconsistent. While he initially referred to the pandemic as a "hoax," he later acknowledged its seriousness and pushed for efforts to accelerate vaccine development. Operation Warp Speed, a public-private partnership aimed at developing and distributing a vaccine, was considered a success in terms of its speed and effectiveness. However, Trump's handling of the pandemic did little to reassure the American public, and his approval ratings dropped significantly as the crisis worsened.

A Country Further Divided

The first Trump administration had a profound effect on America. It deepened political polarization, accelerated social divisions, and reshaped the country's economic policies. Trump's presidency was marked by controversy, with many Americans feeling that his leadership style and policies were a departure from traditional norms. While some of his supporters viewed him as a champion of the working class and an outsider who could disrupt the political elite, his critics saw him as a divisive and dangerous figure who undermined democratic institutions.

The long-term impact of the Trump presidency is still unfolding. While some of his policies, such as tax cuts and deregulation, had short-term economic benefits, the broader societal consequences—particularly the intensification of political and racial divisions—may be felt for years to come. Whether his presidency ultimately helped or harmed the country is a question that will continue to be debated for years. However, one thing is certain: the Trump administration left an indelible mark on the United States, and its effects will shape the nation's future for decades to come.

The Biden Years

The Biden administration, which began on January 20, 2021, ushered in a new era for American culture, marked by significant political, social, and cultural shifts. Under President Joe Biden, the U.S. faced a confluence of complex challenges, including the continuing global pandemic, heightened political polarization, a push for racial justice, and economic recovery. The cultural landscape was deeply influenced by these events, as well as by Biden's policies and leadership style.

This essay will explore the changes in American culture during the Biden administration, focusing on the effects of the president's leadership on political discourse, social justice movements, economic priorities, public health, media, and the evolving national identity. As we reflect on the first years of the Biden presidency, we can begin to see how American culture is shifting in response to these various factors, which will likely shape the country for years to come.

1. Political Discourse and Polarization

One of the most notable cultural changes in America during the Biden administration is the evolving state of political discourse. In contrast to the tumultuous and combative political climate of the Trump years, Biden's presidency has been defined by calls for unity, reconciliation, and bipartisanship. However, despite these efforts, the deeply entrenched political polarization that has defined American politics over the past several decades has not disappeared. The deep divide between Republicans and Democrats remains, and cultural divides along partisan lines continue to shape the national conversation.

Biden's rhetoric often emphasizes healing and finding common ground, presenting himself as a figure who can bridge the political divide. He has regularly called for civility in political discourse and has attempted to focus on policy solutions that might appeal to both sides of the political spectrum. However, political polarization has only deepened in some respects. Republicans, particularly those aligned with former President Donald Trump, have continued to challenge Biden's legitimacy, leading to a continuation of the partisan gridlock that was pervasive during the Obama and Trump years.

The cultural impact of this political polarization is most visible in the way Americans engage with news and media. Many individuals are increasingly consuming information through outlets that align with their political beliefs, reinforcing their existing perspectives. Social media has become a platform for partisan commentary, where debates are often heated and uncompromising. As a result, political discussions have become more fraught, and common ground is often elusive.

Political Identity and the Rise of Extremism

Political extremism has grown more visible during the Biden administration, and incidents like the January 6, 2021 Capitol insurrection, in which a mob of pro-Trump supporters stormed the U.S. Capitol to prevent the certification of Biden's election, have highlighted the deep fissures in American political culture. The event was a stark reminder of the growing radicalization in American politics, and while Biden has worked to emphasize democratic norms, his presidency has also been marked by the challenge of addressing the threat posed by far-right extremist groups, conspiracy theorists, and anti-government militias.

On the other hand, the cultural response from the left has been one of resistance against the perceived authoritarianism of the Trump administration and efforts to preserve democratic principles. This ideological polarization has only intensified during the Biden years, particularly around issues such as voting rights, the treatment of immigrants, and the ongoing battles over the legitimacy of the 2020 election.

2. Social Justice Movements and Racial Equity

A defining feature of the Biden administration has been its response to racial injustice and social equity. The cultural shifts in America in recent years, especially following the murder of George Floyd in 2020, have driven a renewed national reckoning with racism and inequality. Biden has made addressing racial equity a priority, and his presidency has brought discussions of race and justice to the forefront of American politics and culture.

The Black Lives Matter Movement

The Black Lives Matter (BLM) movement has seen continued momentum under Biden's leadership. The movement, which advocates for an end to police violence and systemic racism, gained widespread attention following the murder of George Floyd and the subsequent nationwide protests. Biden, who campaigned on promises to address racial injustice, has made several policy proposals aimed at addressing inequality. These have included calls for police reform, investments in communities of color, and a commitment to advancing voting rights.

However, progress on these issues has been slow, as many of Biden's proposed reforms have faced resistance in Congress. Despite this, the cultural impact of BLM has been undeniable. It has not only changed the way many Americans think about race and policing but has also brought issues of racial justice to the forefront of the public consciousness. In addition, BLM has sparked a wider conversation about the history of racism in America and has encouraged critical examination of symbols, monuments, and institutions that uphold white supremacy.

Biden's Commitment to Equity and Inclusion

Biden has taken steps to advance racial equity through his executive orders and appointments. Early in his presidency, he signed an executive order directing the federal government to prioritize equity in policy-making, aiming to reduce disparities in areas such as housing, education, and healthcare. His administration has also made history by appointing a diverse array of individuals to key positions, including the first female vice president, Kamala Harris, and a record number of women and people of color to his cabinet and staff.

One of the most significant social cultural changes during Biden's administration is the increasing mainstream visibility of marginalized groups. The focus on gender equity, LGBTQ+ rights, and the treatment of Indigenous communities has grown, in part due to Biden's commitment to inclusivity and justice. As part of this, there has been a larger push to increase visibility for marginalized voices and challenge systems of oppression across multiple sectors, including the entertainment industry, corporate America, and education.

3. COVID-19 and Public Health Culture

The COVID-19 pandemic profoundly affected American culture during the first year of Biden's administration. The pandemic, which continued into 2021, fundamentally altered everyday life for millions of Americans. With the arrival of vaccines and a more coordinated federal response under Biden, the cultural landscape began to shift toward recovery, but the impact of the pandemic on American life cannot be understated.

Biden's Response to the Pandemic

From the start of his presidency, Biden made combatting the pandemic his top priority. His administration implemented the largest vaccination campaign in American history, with the goal of vaccinating millions of Americans in a matter of months. The vaccine rollout, though initially slow, accelerated as production ramped up and distribution channels were expanded. Under Biden's leadership, there was a greater focus on science-based policy and expert guidance, which helped restore public confidence in the CDC and other health agencies.

However, cultural divides around the pandemic response persisted. Mask mandates, lockdowns, and vaccine requirements became deeply politicized, with some Americans resisting public health measures due to political or ideological reasons. These cultural divides have influenced public opinion on government intervention, and the pandemic highlighted ongoing challenges related to public trust in health authorities. Biden's leadership has worked to center expert advice, but the ideological divide on pandemic management remains a major issue.

Mental Health and the Pandemic

The pandemic has had a profound impact on Americans' mental health. Social isolation, economic instability, and the uncertainty of the virus have taken a toll on many people's psychological well-being. Under Biden's leadership, mental health has received increased attention, with the administration prioritizing access to mental health services and acknowledging the widespread emotional and psychological strain caused by the pandemic.

The cultural impact of this is reflected in a growing conversation about mental health in American society. The stigma surrounding mental health issues has been gradually breaking down, with more Americans feeling empowered to seek help and discuss their struggles openly. Biden has been a vocal advocate for improving mental health care access and addressing the mental health crisis exacerbated by COVID-19.

4. Economic and Cultural Shifts: The American Worker

The cultural landscape of America during the Biden administration has also been shaped by the president's economic policies, particularly those aimed at alleviating the financial strain caused by the pandemic. Biden's administration has focused on addressing income inequality, expanding access to healthcare, and promoting a more equitable economic recovery.

The American Rescue Plan

In March 2021, Biden signed the American Rescue Plan Act into law, a $1.9 trillion stimulus package designed to provide immediate relief to Americans struggling during the pandemic. The plan provided direct payments to individuals, extended unemployment benefits, and increased funding for vaccine distribution. The plan also included provisions to help small businesses and provide support for schools, which had struggled to adapt to remote learning.

The cultural significance of this economic intervention was considerable. It represented a shift toward more progressive economic policies, with an emphasis on addressing income inequality and supporting working-class Americans. For many Americans, particularly those hit hardest by the pandemic, the direct financial assistance provided by the American Rescue Plan was a lifeline that helped mitigate the cultural and economic damage caused by the crisis.

Labor and Workers' Rights

Under Biden's leadership, there has been a cultural shift towards greater advocacy for workers' rights and labor protections. As part of his broader economic agenda, Biden has called for raising the federal minimum wage to $15 per hour and improving labor standards. His administration has also taken steps to expand access to paid family and sick leave, strengthen collective bargaining rights, and promote workplace safety.

The cultural shift toward labor advocacy has been reflected in the growing visibility of labor movements, particularly in industries such as retail, food service, and technology. Strikes, union organizing efforts, and protests for better working conditions have become more prominent during Biden's presidency, signaling a renewed interest in workers' rights and labor solidarity.

5. Cultural Shifts in Media and Technology

The cultural landscape of the Biden administration has also been shaped by the continued evolution of media and technology. In many ways, the presidency has occurred in a highly mediated environment, with social media, cable news, and digital platforms playing an increasingly central role in shaping public opinion.

Social Media and Disinformation

The rise of misinformation and disinformation, particularly on social media platforms like Facebook, Twitter, and YouTube, has had a significant cultural impact. Under the Biden administration, there has been a continued battle to address the spread of false information, particularly around the COVID-19 pandemic, the 2020 election, and issues of racial justice. The culture of online discourse has become increasingly polarized, with social media serving as both a platform for activism and a space for the spread of conspiracy theories.

Biden's administration has taken steps to tackle the problem of disinformation, including efforts to engage with tech companies to address false claims and the role of social media in amplifying extremist ideologies. However, the cultural influence of social media remains a challenge, as it continues to shape public discourse and influence political behavior.

6. A Changing National Identity

As a whole, the Biden administration has contributed to a shift in American national identity. While the cultural divisions that characterized the Trump era remain, Biden's presidency has centered on themes of unity, resilience, and the need for collective action in the face of crises. The challenges of the pandemic, racial injustice, and economic inequality have forced Americans to reckon with their shared future in ways that may have seemed distant in the past.

Biden's emphasis on democracy, international cooperation, and the protection of democratic institutions also marks a return to a more traditional vision of American exceptionalism, one rooted in values of fairness, liberty, and equality. While the country remains divided, the cultural shifts of Biden's administration point to a reimagining of the national identity in which inclusivity, equity, and a commitment to the rule of law play a central role.

The cultural changes in America during the Biden administration reflect the complexities of a country in flux. From political polarization and social justice movements to the challenges posed by the pandemic and economic inequality, Biden's presidency has been a time of reckoning and redefinition. While many of the issues that have shaped American culture during his presidency are deeply entrenched and will take time to resolve, the Biden administration's policies and leadership have undeniably influenced the cultural landscape, leading to shifts in how Americans engage with politics, race, economics, and national identity.

These cultural shifts will likely continue to unfold throughout Biden's presidency and beyond, as the country confronts ongoing challenges and opportunities for growth. The legacy of the Biden administration, from a cultural perspective, will be shaped not only by the policy outcomes it achieves but also by the broader societal shifts that are taking place during this transformative time in American history.

The Second Run

The 2024 American Presidential Election: A Comprehensive Analysis

The 2024 American presidential election was a pivotal moment in the history of the United States. Coming on the heels of the tumultuous 2020 election and the subsequent political climate shaped by the Trump presidency, the 2024 election served as a referendum on the state of American democracy, the country's political ideologies, and the direction it wished to take moving forward. Several factors, including the political landscape, party dynamics, key issues, and potential candidates, shapes the outcome of the election, and understanding these elements provides valuable insight into the path ahead for the United States.

Key factors influenced the 2024 election, such as the ongoing legacy of the Trump administration, the shifting political ideologies of both major political parties, the role of key issues, the candidates for both the Republican and Democratic parties, and the potential impact of voter demographics. We will also take a look at the potential challenges and opportunities in the election process itself, from voting rights to election security and beyond.

1. The Political Landscape: A Country Divided

The United States in 2024 will remain a deeply divided nation. The aftermath of the 2020 election, which saw Joe Biden defeat incumbent President Donald Trump in a highly contentious race, set the stage for a continuation of the partisan polarization that has come to define American politics in the 21st century. Under Trump, American politics became increasingly fractured, with deep ideological divides between liberals and conservatives, urban and rural populations, and coastal versus heartland states. This polarization continues to shape the political discourse.

Trump's presidency, his loss in 2020, and his continued influence over the Republican Party will all be defining elements of his administration.

On the other side, President Joe Biden's approval rating had been a topic of debate throughout his presidency. While he entered office with high hopes of uniting the country after Trump's tenure, his time in office was marked by challenges related to the ongoing pandemic, economic recovery, and political gridlock. His ability to address key issues like healthcare, climate change, and immigration factored heavily into his prospects for re-election and his party's chances of holding onto the presidency. Kamala Harris, his successor as candidate, was seen as nothing more than an extension of the Biden Administration. For matters of this argument, we will concentrate on the policies that she was made to defend.

2. The Role of the Economy: Recovery and Recession

The state of the American economy undoubtedly played a major role in shaping the outcome of the 2024 election. As of 2021, the U.S. economy had been in the process of recovery from the devastating impacts of the COVID-19 pandemic. The Biden administration pursued a large-scale economic stimulus plan, including the American Rescue Plan, designed to provide financial relief to individuals, businesses, and healthcare systems. Additionally, Biden's infrastructure bill aimed to revitalize America's infrastructure, boost job creation, and address the growing need for modernization in transportation, energy, and technology.

While these initiatives helped spur economic growth, the nation still faced significant challenges. Supply chain issues, inflation, labor shortages, and rising housing prices were just a few of the economic obstacles that weighed heavily on the electorate's perception of the administration's handling of the economy. The economic trajectory heading into the 2024 election was a central issue, and any signs of economic instability hurt Harris's election prospects.

Presidents historically benefit from periods of economic expansion, and the voters' perception of the economy—whether through employment rates, wage growth, or economic inequality—have a lasting impact on their decision. In this case all economic factors were good, but a combination of corporate media bias and disinformation campaigns skewed the public opinion about the reality of the American economy. (More on that later.)

Economic inequality remains a contentious issue. While Biden's administration prioritized addressing wealth disparity through progressive policies such as increased taxation on the wealthy and expanding social safety nets, Republicans largely opposed these measures, favoring tax cuts and deregulation as ways to stimulate growth.

3. Climate Change: A Growing Political Issue

Climate change has become one of the most pressing issues facing the world today. Its growing importance in American politics is reflected in the fact that both major parties had to address the issue in the 2024 election, whether through policy proposals or party rhetoric.

Under the Biden administration, the U.S. rejoined the Paris Agreement, signaling a commitment to international efforts to combat climate change. Biden proposed several green energy initiatives aimed at transitioning to a carbon-neutral economy, including plans for clean energy investments and environmental regulations. However, climate change remains a contentious issue, particularly in regions of the country where industries like oil and gas remain critical to local economies.

For the Democratic Party, climate change is increasingly being framed as an existential crisis that demands urgent action. Progressive candidates will likely advocate for aggressive climate policies that include the Green New Deal, expanded renewable energy infrastructure, and carbon emissions reductions. Environmental justice is also becoming a key area of focus, with Democrats aiming to address the disproportionate impact of environmental degradation on low-income and minority communities.

On the other hand, After his inaugeration, Donald Trump immeiately removed the United States from the Paris Agreement and many Republicans continue to downplay the severity of climate change or frame it as a partisan issue rather than a global threat. The party has historically favored policies that support the fossil fuel industry, and many Republican candidates in 2024 advocated for more limited government intervention in the energy market, arguing that such policies harm businesses and job creators.

The 2024 election reflected the growing tension between those advocating for aggressive climate action and those who view such efforts as too costly or burdensome. Voters' attitudes toward climate change will likely continue to be a deciding factor in future races, especially in swing states like Florida, Texas, and Pennsylvania, where environmental concerns intersect with economic priorities.

4. Healthcare: A Core Issue for American Voters

Healthcare has been a central issue in American politics for many years. The Affordable Care Act (ACA), also known as Obamacare, remains one of the signature legislative achievements of the Obama administration and a key point of contention in American politics. Under President Biden, the ACA has been preserved, and the administration has expanded access to healthcare through enhanced subsidies and the expansion of Medicaid in many states.

However, healthcare remains a contentious issue, particularly with regard to the rising costs of prescription drugs, insurance premiums, and the overall affordability of healthcare. Biden's "Build Back Better" agenda proposed measures aimed at lowering prescription drug prices and increasing access to affordable healthcare, but these proposals have been stymied by resistance from Republicans and moderate Democrats. The debate over Medicare for All versus private healthcare options remains unresolved within the Democratic Party, and it is likely that this divide will continue to shape the discourse.

For Republicans, healthcare policy will continue to be a focal point, with many calling for the repeal of the ACA and advocating for a more market-driven approach. While there is growing support within the GOP for addressing healthcare costs, there is no unified plan as to how this should be accomplished. This lack of clarity on healthcare policy is a disadvantage to the current administration.

Americans once again face the question of whether to expand the social safety net through government intervention in healthcare or to lean toward market-based reforms that reduce government involvement. The healthcare debate will likely continue to shape the electoral preferences of key demographic groups, especially those in the working class and rural America, where healthcare access and affordability are often major concerns.

5. The Candidates: Contenders and Key Figures

Democratic Candidates: Biden and Beyond

Joe Biden's approval rating has fluctuated, he remains a popular figure within the Democratic Party, particularly among older voters and moderates. But the Harrris candidacy faced challenges from more progressive Democrats, who felt that the Biden administration had not been bold enough in pushing for reforms on issues like healthcare, climate change, and economic inequality.

Kamala Harris's, visibility and political clout were expected to grow in the years leading up to the election, but sh3e was largely kept in the shadows. This proved to be a disadvasntage when she became the nominated candidate. Her identity as the first woman of color to hold the vice presidency and her background as a progressive leader should have made her a formidable candidate in 2024.

Other potential Democratic candidates included Senators Bernie Sanders and Elizabeth Warren, both of whom have maintained a strong base of progressive support. Governors like Gavin Newsom of California and Andrew Cuomo of New York had also been mentioned as possible contenders. However, the left-wing base was left with little time after a presidential debate debacle in which Joe Biden seemed weak and incompetent. Democrats needed a candidate who was more aligned with their policy preferences, especially when it came to healthcare and climate change. What they got was a relative unknown who did not seem to fully support the administration to which she belonged.

Republican Candidates: Trump and only Trump

Donald Trump, despite losing the 2020 election, remained a dominant force within the Republican Party. His influence over the party, especially among grassroots conservatives and MAGA supporters, cannot be overstated. Trump's actions and rhetoric faced little opposition within the party, as many Republican leaders remained loyal to him.

However, Trump's candidacy was not without controversy. Some Republicans, particularly establishment figures, had begun to distance themselves from Trump, believing that his polarizing nature could hurt the party's chances in the general election. In this context, potential challengers to Trump in the Republican primaries might have included figures like Florida Governor Ron DeSantis, Texas Senator Ted Cruz, and former UN Ambassador Nikki Haley. These candidates were seen as more establishment-friendly alternatives to Trump, and they could have made their case to Republican voters by focusing on issues like the economy, immigration, and national security.

The Republican Party in 2024 was a weak battle between the Trump wing of the party and a more traditional conservative faction, each trying to assert its vision for the future of the nation. Trump had the backing of several billionaires, media moguls, and tech companies. Trump won the nomination.

6. Voter Demographics: Changing Trends and Critical Swing States

Voter demographics played a crucial role in determining the outcome of the 2024 election. Over the past few decades, America's demographic landscape has shifted significantly, with an increasing percentage of voters coming from younger generations, communities of color, and urban areas. These demographic shifts have made certain states, such as Arizona, Georgia, and Pennsylvania, increasingly competitive.

Voter turnout and engagement was key. In 2020, turnout reached historic levels, and the 2024 election saw similar levels of engagement, particularly among younger voters and people of color. The Republican Party's stance on voting rights was a major factor, with various state legislatures pushing to enact restrictive voting laws, which depressed turnout in some areas. These efforts in any other election might have prompted significant legal challenges and public debates about the integrity of the electoral process.

7. Challenges and Opportunities: The Electoral Process

Election security and voter access were important issues in the 2024 election. In the aftermath of the 2020 election, there were widespread claims of voter fraud, which were largely debunked but fueled a continuing debate over the integrity of the electoral system. The aftermath of the Capitol riot, which was driven by Trump's refusal to accept the results of the election, was a critical issue. Trump again complained in advance that the vote would not be legitimate if he were to lose. Those issues were immediately dropped by his party the day after the election.

Questions about the legitimacy of the election remain. Republicans control all three branches of the government as a result, and no further action will be taken.

How America Has Been Affected

The political environment in the United States today is deeply complex, marked by polarization, inequality, changing societal values, and challenges both domestically and internationally. The country is facing multiple critical issues, ranging from political polarization to economic inequality, from social justice movements to international tensions. These dynamics are compounded by changes in the media landscape, shifting voter demographics, and the ongoing influence of technology. In this context, the political environment is not only influenced by policy debates but by the broader culture and the nation's evolving understanding of democracy, rights, and governance.

1. Political Polarization: A Nation Divided

One of the defining characteristics of the American political environment in recent years has been increasing polarization. This divide manifests in multiple ways: partisan animosity, geographic divisions, and ideological extremism. Polarization in the U.S. has deepened over the past several decades, but it has become particularly pronounced since the 2010s, with sharp divides between Democrats and Republicans, urban and rural communities, and various demographic groups. Economic inequality further deepens the divide.

The Rise of Partisan Politics

The roots of this political polarization can be traced to several factors, including the growing ideological homogeneity of both the Republican and Democratic parties. The Democratic Party has shifted leftward on many issues, particularly social justice, healthcare, and environmental policy. The Republican Party, meanwhile, has increasingly embraced conservative populism, particularly since the rise of Donald Trump.

This shift toward populism has made it harder for the two parties to find common ground, especially on issues like immigration, healthcare, and taxation.

In the years following the 2008 financial crisis and the election of Barack Obama, political gridlock became more common in Washington, D.C., with both parties entrenched in their positions. The era of cooperation that characterized earlier American politics seemed to have ended, replaced by fierce battles over issues such as the Affordable Care Act, gun control, and the scope of government regulation. Trump's election in 2016 further deepened this divide, as his style of governance, based on populism and often divisive rhetoric, reinforced the animosity between the left and right.

Impact of Social Media

Social media has also played a significant role in fueling political polarization. Platforms like Facebook, Twitter, and YouTube amplify partisan viewpoints, creating echo chambers where individuals are exposed primarily to information that reinforces their beliefs. These platforms have been criticized for facilitating the spread of misinformation, fake news, and conspiracy theories, all of which have further divided the American public. The algorithms behind these platforms prioritize engagement, often promoting content that is more sensational and divisive. As a result, many Americans consume news through ideological lenses, deepening divisions in both their political views and their understanding of reality.

The role of social media in politics was particularly pronounced during the 2016 and 2020 presidential elections, where misinformation and foreign interference created lasting impacts on the public's perception of electoral integrity. The 2020 election saw widespread claims of voter fraud and an ongoing battle over mail-in voting, leading to a tense and contentious atmosphere around the results.

Ideological Extremism and the Threat of Violence

The rise of ideological extremism, particularly on the far-right, is another critical aspect of the current political environment. In recent years, American politics has seen an uptick in violent political rhetoric and extremism. The 2021 Capitol insurrection, in which a mob of Trump supporters stormed the U.S. Capitol in an effort to overturn the results of the 2020 presidential election, was a stark reminder of the dangers of political violence and the deepening ideological divide.

Far-right groups, such as militia organizations and white nationalist groups, have been emboldened by populist rhetoric, contributing to a volatile political climate. At the same time, the left has seen the rise of progressive activists pushing for significant social, racial, and economic change. While the left-wing movements have largely focused on nonviolent forms of protest, they too have been subject to criticism from conservatives who see these movements as radical or even destabilizing. The challenge, then, is to navigate the space between these extreme ideological positions while ensuring that democratic norms are upheld and that violence does not become a routine part of political expression.

2. The Biden Administration: Governance and Challenges

In 2021, President Joe Biden assumed office at a time of immense political and social turmoil. The election of Biden marked a shift away from the Trump administration, which had pushed the U.S. further to the right on several key issues. Biden, a moderate Democrat, ran on a platform of unity and healing, attempting to bridge the divides that had grown during the Trump years. However, his presidency has been defined by several crises, including the COVID-19 pandemic, economic instability, racial justice movements, corporate greed, and foreign policy challenges.

The COVID-19 Pandemic

The pandemic was a central issue in Biden's presidency. The virus itself and the political handling of the crisis by the previous administration left the nation in a vulnerable state. Biden's approach to the pandemic was science-driven, with an emphasis on vaccine distribution, mask mandates, and social distancing measures. His administration's success in ramping up the vaccine rollout helped stabilize the situation, but the pandemic revealed deep social, economic, and political divisions.

COVID-19 also laid bare systemic inequities in the U.S., particularly regarding healthcare access, racial disparities in health outcomes, and economic inequalities. The pandemic disproportionately impacted low-income communities and communities of color, further highlighting the challenges Biden's administration faces in addressing inequality.

Economic Recovery and Stimulus

Biden's economic recovery package, the American Rescue Plan, aimed to provide financial relief to individuals, businesses, and state governments. The package included direct payments to Americans, extended unemployment benefits, and support for businesses struggling due to lockdown measures. Additionally, Biden's infrastructure bill, which passed in 2021, is designed to invest in the nation's roads, bridges, broadband, and clean energy sectors.

However, the recovery was slow, and inflation became a significant concern heading into 2024. Rising prices for food, gas, and housing have put pressure on the Biden administration and fueled discontent among voters. While the job market has shown signs of recovery, the economy remains vulnerable to new disruptions, including ongoing supply chain issues and potential future pandemics or natural disasters.

Racial Justice and Social Movements

Biden's presidency has been shaped by a renewed focus on racial justice and addressing systemic inequalities. The murder of George Floyd in 2020 sparked widespread protests and calls for police reform, leading to a national conversation about race, policing, and inequality. Biden campaigned on addressing these issues, and his administration has made moves to prioritize racial equity, including establishing a task force on racial justice and signing executive orders aimed at advancing diversity and inclusion in government.

Despite Biden's rhetoric around racial justice, progress on these issues has been slow, particularly on police reform. Legislation like the George Floyd Justice in Policing Act, which seeks to reform policing practices, has stalled in Congress due to partisan opposition. The slow pace of change on racial issues has frustrated many activists, particularly in communities of color, who feel that their concerns are not being addressed with the urgency they require.

Foreign Policy Challenges

Biden's foreign policy has focused on restoring alliances and reasserting American leadership on the global stage. His administration has taken a more multilateral approach to foreign relations, in contrast to Trump's "America First" stance. Biden's decision to rejoin the Paris Agreement and his efforts to negotiate a nuclear deal with Iran signal a return to diplomacy as a core component of U.S. foreign policy.

However, Biden's foreign policy has faced significant challenges. The chaotic withdrawal from Afghanistan in August 2021 severely damaged the administration's credibility abroad. The Taliban's rapid takeover of the country following the U.S. military's withdrawal was seen as a failure in U.S. strategy and a blow to American influence. Additionally, tensions with China and Russia have escalated, particularly over trade, cybersecurity, and human rights issues. Biden will need to navigate these complex international relationships while maintaining domestic stability and addressing global security concerns.

3. Social Justice Movements: A New Cultural Landscape

Beyond traditional political battles, the U.S. is undergoing significant cultural and societal shifts, particularly around issues of race, gender, and inequality. The Black Lives Matter movement, LGBTQ+ rights, and the #MeToo movement are all powerful forces in the cultural and political landscape, influencing policy debates and shaping public opinion.

Black Lives Matter and Racial Justice

The Black Lives Matter movement, which gained significant traction following the murder of George Floyd, has continued to advocate for an end to systemic racism, particularly in policing. The movement has influenced local and national conversations about police reform, racial profiling, and the criminal justice system. Despite progress in some areas, such as police department reforms in certain cities, significant challenges remain. Structural racism continues to be a pervasive issue in American society, and many activists argue that the government has not done enough to address it.

The Biden administration's focus on racial equity has helped keep the issue in the public eye, but the effectiveness of his policies in addressing racial disparities remains a subject of debate. The intersection of race and economics, particularly regarding wealth inequality and access to education, healthcare, and housing, remains a critical issue for many communities of color.

Gender and LGBTQ+ Rights

Gender and LGBTQ+ rights have also become central political issues, particularly under the Biden administration. Biden has appointed the first openly transgender person to a Cabinet position (Dr. Rachel Levine as Assistant Secretary of Health), signifying a commitment to LGBTQ+ inclusion. Additionally, the administration has signaled its support for expanding protections against discrimination for LGBTQ+ individuals, particularly in healthcare and employment.

However, challenges remain, especially at the state level, where several Republican-led states have passed laws restricting transgender rights, including access to healthcare and participation in sports. These laws have sparked significant national debates about gender identity, freedom of choice, and the role of government in regulating personal lives.

Immigration and Border Control

Immigration continues to be a major flashpoint in U.S. politics. The Biden administration has faced criticism from both sides of the political spectrum. Progressives have pushed for comprehensive immigration reform, including a path to citizenship for undocumented immigrants and expanded protections for asylum seekers. On the other hand, conservatives have decried what they see as weak enforcement of border laws and the continued influx of migrants from Central America.

Biden's reversal of many of Trump's immigration policies, such as the "Remain in Mexico" policy, has led to a surge in border crossings, further fueling the debate. The administration's handling of immigration was a significant issue in the 2024 election, with both parties positioning themselves as defenders of national security or champions of immigrant rights.

4. The Role of Technology and Media

Technology and media play an increasingly prominent role in the political environment. Social media platforms, cable news, and digital streaming services all shape public discourse, allowing for the rapid spread of information—and misinformation. The role of social media in elections, particularly the 2020 presidential race, highlighted the power of these platforms to influence public opinion and electoral outcomes.

However, the media landscape is fragmented, with Americans increasingly consuming news that aligns with their political views. This has contributed to a further polarization of the electorate, with individuals on both sides of the political spectrum living in separate information bubbles. The rise of conspiracy theories and fake news, facilitated by social media and online forums, has led to questions about the integrity of democratic elections and the health of American democracy.

5. The Future of American Democracy

As we look ahead to the future of American politics, questions about the resilience of democracy itself loom large. The events of January 6, 2021, when a violent mob of Trump supporters stormed the Capitol in an attempt to overturn the results of the 2020 election, serve as a reminder of how fragile democratic institutions can be when under assault. Efforts to undermine trust in the electoral system, combined with the spread of misinformation, have eroded faith in democratic processes.

As America navigates the current political climate, the health of its democracy will be a central concern. Whether the country can overcome its divisions, restore trust in its institutions, and continue to build an inclusive and just society will depend on the willingness of political leaders and citizens alike to find common ground and work toward shared solutions.

The political environment in the United States today is shaped by deep divisions, ongoing cultural shifts, and significant challenges on both domestic and global fronts. From the legacy of Trumpism to the rise of progressive movements, from economic recovery efforts to racial justice battles, the country finds itself at a crossroads. The way forward will require a nuanced understanding of these political dynamics, as well as a commitment to democratic values, inclusivity, and responsible governance.

The Role of Mainstream Media in American Elections

Mainstream media plays a critical role in shaping the political landscape and influencing public opinion in the United States, particularly during elections. The media serves as the primary channel through which information about candidates, political platforms, policies, and events is disseminated to the public. Over the years, the relationship between the media and American elections has evolved significantly, from a highly centralized, print-based model to a more fragmented, digital-driven system. Despite these changes, the core function of the media in elections has remained consistent: to inform, educate, and influence voters.

The multifaceted role of mainstream media in American elections has made it the equivalent of an unofficial branch of US government. Media shapes political discourse. Media bias influences voter behavior, the increasing role of social media, and the ways in which the media's portrayal of candidates and issues impact election outcomes. The challenges facing mainstream media, include concerns over misinformation, media consolidation, and the changing media landscape.

1. Media as the Informational Backbone of Elections

The media's primary function in any democracy is to provide information to the public, allowing citizens to make informed decisions. In the context of American elections, mainstream media—comprising television networks, newspapers, and online outlets—becomes the key vehicle for voters to learn about candidates, political parties, and important issues.

Campaign Coverage and Political Narratives

Throughout an election cycle, mainstream media outlets provide extensive coverage of the candidates, their campaigns, and their platforms. This coverage ranges from straightforward reporting of speeches, debates, and policy proposals to more interpretive content like op-eds, analysis, and commentary. The media's portrayal of candidates often shapes how the public perceives them. A candidate's strengths and weaknesses are often amplified by media outlets, which can influence voter perceptions and opinions.

For instance, during the 2016 presidential election, media outlets focused extensively on Donald Trump's controversial statements, rallies, and personality traits. The saturation of Trump's media presence during the election cycle contributed significantly to his rise in popularity. However, it was not just his controversial actions that gained media attention. His media-savvy ability to use the press to his advantage played a significant role in keeping him in the public eye, despite various controversies.

Similarly, coverage of Hillary Clinton's campaign emphasized her establishment ties and focus on policy details. Media portrayal of her as the "inevitable" nominee and the scrutiny surrounding her use of a private email server during her tenure as Secretary of State played a central role in her 2016 campaign narrative. The media's focus on these issues became a defining feature of her campaign coverage, contributing to the narrative of her candidacy as deeply flawed in the eyes of many voters.

The media also plays a pivotal role in defining the political narratives of an election. The framing of issues like healthcare, immigration, or climate change can significantly influence how voters prioritize these topics when casting their ballots. In 2020, for example, the COVID-19 pandemic dominated much of the media coverage, shaping the political discourse surrounding the election and the candidates' response to the crisis. Joe Biden's emphasis on science and public health became a central message of his campaign, contrasting with Donald Trump's handling of the pandemic.

Debates, Interviews, and Political Advertising

Televised presidential debates are a key aspect of election campaigns in the United States, and the media's role in facilitating and broadcasting these events is central to the election process. Debates offer candidates the opportunity to present their policies directly to the public, and the media's framing of these events often shapes how candidates' performances are perceived. The way the media covers debates—highlighting gaffes, memorable moments, or strong performances—can have a lasting impact on the election's outcome. A particularly strong or weak debate performance can either elevate a candidate or erode their standing with voters.

Interviews and appearances on news programs also provide candidates with opportunities to communicate directly with voters. These interviews are often edited, curated, and presented in ways that influence how the public perceives a candidate's sincerity, competence, and charisma. The media's ability to amplify or downplay specific moments from these appearances has a direct impact on how voters engage with the candidates.

Political advertisements are another integral part of modern campaigns, and mainstream media outlets—particularly television and digital platforms—serve as the primary venues for these ads. Political advertising has become a multi-billion dollar industry in American elections, with campaigns investing heavily in ad buys to reach potential voters. The media's ability to provide platforms for these ads allows campaigns to directly target specific demographics and sway public opinion.

The power of political advertising is magnified by the way it is delivered. The media's role in controlling how and when these ads air can influence the timing of the political message. For example, ads aired during prime-time television shows or highly viewed sporting events can reach millions of viewers in a short period, magnifying the impact of the ad.

2. Media Bias and its Impact on Elections

The issue of media bias has long been a contentious one in American elections. Mainstream media outlets have been accused of having liberal or conservative biases, which can influence how they cover political candidates and issues. While many news organizations maintain editorial standards to ensure fairness, objectivity, and accuracy, biases—whether conscious or unconscious—can still shape how stories are framed and which stories are given prominence.

Liberal vs. Conservative Bias

The claim that mainstream media has a liberal bias is particularly pronounced among conservative circles. Critics of the media argue that outlets like The New York Times, The Washington Post, and CNN have a left-leaning editorial stance, leading to biased coverage of political events. Examples of this perceived bias often include the coverage of conservative candidates, issues like gun rights or abortion, and the portrayal of right-wing political ideologies.

On the other hand, liberal-leaning media outlets often accuse conservative media outlets, like Fox News, of having a conservative bias. Fox News is frequently criticized for offering a platform to conservative viewpoints while minimizing liberal perspectives. Additionally, the network's commentators, such as Sean Hannity and Tucker Carlson, have been accused of framing news stories in a way that promotes a conservative political agenda.

Media seized on Joe Biden's bad debate night with a vengeance, basically running him out of the race and showing a clear bias. The ratio of appearances in the 2024 election on all mainstream media platforms also disproportionately favored Republicans.

The impact of media bias is significant, especially in an election cycle. When voters only consume media from outlets with a particular ideological slant, they are less likely to encounter diverse perspectives and may become further entrenched in their political views. In an age of increasing media fragmentation, this selective exposure has the potential to deepen political polarization.

The Role of Fact-Checking and Accountability

Fact-checking has become an essential tool in combating media bias, particularly in an era where misinformation and disinformation are rampant. Many mainstream media outlets now employ fact-checkers who assess the accuracy of candidates' statements and claims during debates, interviews, and speeches. Fact-checking serves to hold political figures accountable for falsehoods or misleading statements, helping to inform the electorate.

However, the proliferation of misinformation and the speed with which it spreads—especially through social media—complicates the media's role in holding political figures accountable. Mainstream outlets must balance the need to report breaking news with the responsibility to provide accurate and reliable information, all while navigating the pressure of a 24-hour news cycle.

3. The Influence of Media on Voter Behavior

The media plays a crucial role in shaping voter behavior, influencing how citizens form opinions about candidates and issues. While voters may come to an election with preexisting political views, the media can serve as a powerful tool in shaping their decisions at the ballot box. Several factors contribute to the influence of media on voting behavior, including agenda-setting, framing, priming, and persuasion.

Agenda-Setting and Issue Salience

One of the most important roles that media plays in elections is in agenda-setting. The media has the ability to determine which issues are highlighted during a campaign, which in turn influences the public's perception of what is important. For example, if the media focuses heavily on economic issues such as unemployment or inflation, voters may place greater importance on these issues when deciding which candidate to support.

The media also helps shape the salience of certain issues by emphasizing their importance or making them more visible. For example, if the media devotes extensive coverage to a particular issue—such as healthcare or climate change—voters may view that issue as more important in the context of the election, potentially swaying votes.

The Role of Polls in American Elections

Polls have become an integral part of modern American political campaigns and public life. From predicting election outcomes to shaping public discourse, polling data provides a snapshot of public opinion that political candidates, media, and even voters themselves closely monitor. The role of polls in American elections is vast and multifaceted, impacting everything from strategy to media coverage to the psychological state of voters. This essay will explore the various ways in which polls influence American elections, the methods behind polling, and the potential benefits and drawbacks of this ubiquitous practice in political campaigns.

I. The Evolution of Political Polling in the United States

The practice of polling dates back to the early 20th century, although public opinion surveys in their modern form were not widely used until the 1930s. George Gallup, often credited as the father of modern political polling, pioneered the use of scientific polling techniques in the 1930s. Gallup's approach was groundbreaking because it was based on random sampling, which ensured that his polls were representative of the larger population.

Gallup's methods were a response to the often unreliable and unscientific straw polls that had dominated political discourse in the United States before then. Straw polls, often conducted by newspapers or other media outlets, would solicit opinions from a self-selected group of people, typically leading to biased and inaccurate results. Gallup's approach aimed to correct this by ensuring that poll respondents were selected randomly and represented a cross-section of society.

Since the early days of polling, the practice has expanded and evolved in response to changing technologies and political climates. The introduction of telephone surveys in the mid-20th century, followed by the rise of online polling in the 21st century, has made polling more accessible and widespread. However, as polling has become more sophisticated, so too have the critiques of its methodology and its influence on elections.

II. The Mechanics of Political Polling

At its core, political polling aims to measure the preferences, attitudes, and behaviors of a given population at a specific point in time. Polling agencies typically use a method called random sampling, where they select a group of respondents from a broader population in a way that reflects the demographic makeup of that population. The goal is to ensure that the sample is representative, minimizing the possibility of bias.

Polls are generally conducted using one of two primary methods: telephone interviews or online surveys. Both methods have their advantages and disadvantages. Telephone polls can provide real-time feedback, but they are also subject to limitations, such as a reliance on landlines (which have become increasingly rare) and the potential for respondent bias (for example, older respondents being more likely to answer a landline survey). Online surveys, while able to reach a wider and more diverse audience, can also suffer from selection bias, as they exclude individuals who do not have regular access to the internet.

In addition to sampling methods, polling accuracy is influenced by the way questions are phrased and the timing of the poll. Question wording is crucial because slight changes in how a question is framed can lead to very different results. Additionally, the timing of a poll can impact its accuracy. Public opinion can shift rapidly in response to breaking news events, debates, or scandals, so polling conducted at one moment in time may not reflect the broader trends that develop over the course of a campaign.

Pollsters also calculate a margin of error for each poll, which indicates the degree of uncertainty in the results. The margin of error represents the range within which the true result is likely to fall. For example, if a poll shows a candidate with 50% support, with a margin of error of ±3%, the actual level of support could be anywhere from 47% to 53%. Understanding the margin of error is key for interpreting poll results accurately and recognizing that no poll is perfect.

III. The Role of Polls in Election Campaigns

Polls play a significant role in the strategy of political campaigns. Candidates and their teams rely heavily on polling data to assess the mood of the electorate, adjust their messaging, and allocate resources effectively. The primary goal of polling for a campaign is to understand the preferences of voters and determine the best path to victory.

One of the most important uses of polling in campaigns is identifying battleground states or regions. In the United States, elections are not determined by a national popular vote but by the Electoral College system, where each state is assigned a certain number of electors based on its population. Consequently, the focus of most presidential campaigns is on a small number of key swing states, where the race is expected to be close. Polls can help campaigns target their efforts on the states and regions where they have the greatest chance of winning.

Polls also allow campaigns to fine-tune their messaging. By tracking how voters respond to different messages and policy proposals, campaigns can shift their focus to the issues that resonate most with their target audience. For example, if polling shows that a candidate's stance on healthcare is particularly popular in a certain state, the campaign may choose to emphasize this issue in speeches, ads, and other forms of outreach in that region.

In addition to informing strategy, polls also serve as a tool for gauging the effectiveness of a candidate's campaign. By conducting regular internal polls, campaigns can track how their support levels change over time, adjusting tactics and resources accordingly. For example, if a candidate's favorability rating begins to drop in a critical swing state, the campaign may opt to pivot its messaging or make strategic changes in the field operations.

IV. The Impact of Polls on Voter Behavior

While polls are often used by political campaigns to inform strategy, they also have a direct impact on voters themselves. The presence of polls can influence how people perceive the election, how they decide to vote, and whether they even participate in the process.

One of the most well-documented effects of polls is the "bandwagon effect," where voters are more likely to support a candidate who is perceived as leading in the polls. When a candidate is shown to be ahead, they may attract additional support from voters who want to back a winner. Conversely, the "underdog effect" occurs when voters are motivated to support a candidate who is trailing in the polls, out of a desire to buck the trend or support a perceived outsider.

Polls can also contribute to voter apathy and disengagement. When polls indicate that one candidate is leading by a large margin, some voters may feel that their vote will not make a difference, leading them to stay home on Election Day. On the other hand, a close race can energize voters, leading to higher turnout. The media often plays a significant role in shaping these perceptions by emphasizing close races or dramatic shifts in the polls, which can either increase or decrease voter enthusiasm.

The psychological impact of polls extends to the concept of "strategic voting." In some cases, voters may cast their ballots not for their first-choice candidate, but for a candidate who has a better chance of winning, based on poll numbers. This can result in voters "voting for the lesser evil" or shifting their support to a more viable candidate, rather than their true preferred candidate. Polls can also influence how people evaluate candidates' chances, potentially leading to a self-fulfilling prophecy where voters begin to support the candidate they believe is most likely to win.

V. Polling and the Media

The media plays a critical role in shaping the way polls are disseminated and understood by the public. Poll results are often heavily covered in the media, especially in the lead-up to an election. In many cases, poll numbers become a central part of campaign coverage, influencing both how candidates are perceived and how the election is framed.

Media outlets frequently use polling data to highlight trends in the race, often comparing the standings of different candidates over time. Poll results can dominate news cycles, becoming a key part of the narrative surrounding a particular election. However, the media's focus on polls can also have negative consequences. The heavy emphasis on polling can contribute to a "horse race" mentality, where the focus shifts away from substantive policy discussions and towards the perceived competitiveness of the race.

Polling results can also be used to manipulate public perception. While many reputable polling organizations strive for accuracy and objectivity, some media outlets and political groups may commission polls with the goal of advancing a particular narrative. "Push polls," for example, are designed to sway public opinion by framing questions in a biased manner or by asking leading questions. Such polls, while unethical, can still influence public discourse by disseminating skewed results.

VI. The Limitations and Criticisms of Polling

Despite their widespread use, polling has faced significant criticism, particularly regarding its accuracy and its ability to truly reflect public opinion. One of the major challenges of polling is the phenomenon of "nonresponse bias." As certain segments of the population are more likely to respond to polls than others, the sample may not accurately represent the diversity of views within the electorate. This can lead to skewed results that do not reflect the true preferences of the population.

Another issue is the increasing difficulty of reaching a representative sample. The rise of cell phones, internet usage, and changing demographics has made it harder for pollsters to ensure that their samples are truly representative. Traditional telephone polls, for example, often exclude younger or lower-income individuals who are less likely to have landlines. Online polling, while able to reach a broader audience, still faces challenges in terms of accessibility and the ability to reach hard-to-reach populations.

Polling is also criticized for contributing to the "horse race" mentality in political coverage. By focusing heavily on numbers and rankings, polls can overshadow substantive policy debates, reducing complex issues to simple metrics. Additionally, the focus on polls can encourage the media to cover elections as a contest between personalities rather than an opportunity to address important policy questions.

Finally, polling can be inaccurate. In recent years, several high-profile elections, including the 2016 U.S. presidential election and the 2020 election, have demonstrated that even sophisticated polling methods can fail to predict outcomes accurately. Misleading results, particularly in swing states, have contributed to the growing skepticism about the reliability of polls.

Polls play an essential role in American elections, serving as a tool for both political campaigns and the media. They provide a snapshot of public opinion that helps campaigns craft strategy, allocate resources, and gauge voter sentiment. However, polls also have their limitations, including potential biases, inaccuracies, and the risk of influencing voter behavior in ways that may not reflect the true preferences of the electorate. The growing reliance on polls raises important questions about the accuracy and impact of polling data in modern elections. While polls are likely to remain a fixture in American politics, their role and influence will continue to be a subject of debate and scrutiny in the years to come.

The Role of Churches in American Presidential Elections

The role of religion in American politics has been a defining feature of the nation's history, and religious institutions, particularly churches, have played an influential role in shaping presidential elections throughout the country's development. The intersection of faith and politics in the U.S. is complex, with churches acting as both moral guides for individual behavior and powerful political forces that shape the broader political landscape. In this analysis, we will explore how churches in the United States influence presidential elections, how religious leaders and organizations mobilize voters, the role of faith-based political movements, and the long-standing relationship between church and state.

1. The History of Religious Influence on American Politics

Before delving into the specific role churches play in contemporary elections, it is essential to understand the historical context of religion in American politics. America's founding fathers crafted a political system that sought to balance freedom of religion with the principle of the separation of church and state, enshrined in the First Amendment of the U.S. Constitution. This separation has, over time, allowed for a political landscape in which religious institutions can have a significant influence on political discourse without directly controlling the government.

From the early days of the republic, churches and religious leaders have played a crucial role in shaping public attitudes toward key political issues. During the 19th century, for example, evangelical Protestant leaders were central to the abolitionist movement, advocating for the end of slavery in the South. In the 20th century, churches were also at the forefront of civil rights movements, with religious leaders like Martin Luther King Jr. guiding protests and efforts to secure equal rights for African Americans.

At the same time, the rise of conservative religious movements in the 1980s—particularly the Moral Majority led by Jerry Falwell and other evangelical leaders—transformed American political discourse. This shift marked the emergence of the "Religious Right," a political coalition that sought to influence public policy on issues like abortion, same-sex marriage, and religious freedom.

As the country's demographic and religious composition evolved in the latter half of the 20th century, churches—particularly Protestant, Catholic, and evangelical communities—became key players in national elections, particularly presidential contests.

2. Mobilizing Voters: Churches as Political Actors

One of the most significant ways churches influence American presidential elections is through voter mobilization. Religious congregations often play a key role in encouraging individuals to vote, both through sermons, religious education programs, and grassroots organizing efforts. Churches can serve as powerful spaces for cultivating political engagement, offering moral guidance on political issues, and creating community networks that encourage participation in the electoral process.

Voter Registration and Turnout Efforts

In many cases, churches, especially those with large and loyal congregations, partner with political campaigns or non-partisan voter engagement organizations to encourage voter registration and turnout. During presidential election years, churches may hold voter registration drives or host community events designed to inform voters about the candidates and the issues at stake.

For instance, during the 2008 and 2012 elections, the African American church played a crucial role in mobilizing voters for President Barack Obama. African American churches, particularly those with strong traditions of social justice, were instrumental in registering voters, particularly in battleground states, and encouraging them to vote for a candidate who promised to address issues important to the Black community, such as healthcare reform and criminal justice reform.

Similarly, evangelical Christian churches have been a crucial part of the conservative base that has supported Republican candidates in recent decades. Many evangelical pastors and church leaders have encouraged their congregations to vote based on their values, emphasizing issues such as abortion, traditional marriage, and religious freedom. These efforts have proven to be a significant factor in mobilizing millions of conservative voters, especially in key swing states.

Influencing Political Behavior Through Sermons and Religious Teachings

In addition to more explicit voter mobilization efforts, churches influence the political views and voting behaviors of their members through the messages delivered during sermons and religious education programs. Pastors and church leaders are often viewed as trusted moral guides, and their views on political issues can carry significant weight with their congregations.

Many evangelical pastors, for example, have used their pulpits to speak out on issues such as abortion, same-sex marriage, and religious freedom, often advocating for specific political stances aligned with conservative Christian teachings. In doing so, they have shaped the political ideologies of their congregants, encouraging them to vote in a manner consistent with their faith-based views on these topics.

However, it is important to note that not all religious institutions are politically aligned in the same way. Catholic churches, for example, may take more nuanced positions on political issues, advocating for social justice, economic equality, and the protection of the poor and marginalized. Many liberal Christian leaders and churches emphasize progressive policies related to healthcare, climate change, and poverty alleviation, influencing the voting preferences of their congregations.

While churches do not explicitly endorse political candidates (at least not directly, due to restrictions on tax-exempt organizations), religious leaders are able to impart their political values through religious teachings. This indirect influence can significantly impact voters' choices during presidential elections, as individuals often look to their churches for guidance on moral and social issues.

3. The Religious Right and the Rise of Evangelical Political Power

The Religious Right, which emerged as a political force in the 1980s, represents one of the most powerful and visible ways in which churches have influenced presidential elections in the United States. The movement was initially galvanized by a coalition of conservative Christians—particularly evangelical Protestants—who were motivated by concerns about issues like abortion, the role of religion in public life, and the perceived erosion of traditional family values.

Jerry Falwell and the Moral Majority

A central figure in the rise of the Religious Right was Jerry Falwell, an influential pastor and founder of the Moral Majority, a political organization that sought to unite conservative Christians behind a set of shared values. The Moral Majority played a significant role in mobilizing evangelical Christians to vote in the 1980 presidential election, where Republican candidate Ronald Reagan defeated incumbent Jimmy Carter. Falwell and other religious leaders framed Reagan as the candidate who would best defend Christian values and promote conservative policies on issues such as abortion and school prayer.

The success of the Religious Right in the 1980s marked a turning point in American politics, as it demonstrated the growing influence of churches and religious voters in presidential elections. Reagan's victory was in part the result of a strong turnout among evangelical Christians, who became a crucial constituency for the Republican Party.

Impact on Republican Politics and Subsequent Elections

The influence of the Religious Right has been a defining feature of Republican presidential campaigns ever since. Candidates like George H.W. Bush, George W. Bush, and Donald Trump have all sought to court evangelical Christian voters, recognizing the importance of this demographic in key battleground states. The Bush family, in particular, capitalized on their strong evangelical support, with George W. Bush securing a significant portion of the evangelical vote in both his 2000 and 2004 campaigns. His stance on issues like abortion, same-sex marriage, and religious freedom helped solidify his appeal to conservative Christians.

Donald Trump, despite his controversial background and statements, also successfully appealed to evangelical voters in the 2016 and 2020 elections. His promises to appoint conservative judges, protect religious freedoms, and support traditional family values resonated deeply with many evangelical Christians. Trump's ability to secure the backing of key religious leaders, such as Jerry Falwell Jr. and Franklin Graham, played a central role in mobilizing religious conservatives to support his candidacy.

The strength of the Religious Right has meant that Republican candidates must actively engage with religious voters and align themselves with religious values in order to maintain support among this key constituency.

4. The Role of African American Churches in Presidential Elections

African American churches have long been central to political life in Black communities, serving as spaces for social and political organizing. These churches have been influential in shaping presidential elections, particularly in recent decades. The history of African American churches' involvement in politics can be traced back to the Civil Rights Movement, when religious leaders such as Martin Luther King Jr. played pivotal roles in advocating for racial equality and justice.

Barack Obama and the Black Church

The election of Barack Obama in 2008 marked a watershed moment for African American churches in politics. Obama's candidacy was buoyed by strong support from Black voters, who were mobilized by African American churches. These churches became key sites for voter registration drives, fundraising, and political activism, particularly in key swing states like Ohio, Michigan, and Pennsylvania.

Obama's campaign also spoke directly to the legacy of the Black church, with his messages of hope and change resonating deeply with African American congregants. His candidacy was seen by many as the culmination of years of civil rights activism, and his ability to connect with Black voters through religious and cultural channels was a defining feature of his 2008 and 2012 campaigns.

Religious leaders in African American churches were instrumental in helping Obama secure a historic victory in 2008, and their support continued to be critical in 2012. Obama's faith-based outreach efforts, including his partnership with faith-based organizations, helped to solidify his connection with religious communities and further mobilize Black voters.

5. The Politics of Religious Identity in Modern Elections

In recent years, the role of religion in American presidential elections has become more complex, as the nation's religious landscape has evolved. While evangelical Protestants and African American churches remain key players, the growing diversity of the U.S. population has led to increased attention on other religious groups, including Catholic voters, Jewish Americans, and Muslims.

Catholic voters, in particular, have been a pivotal swing demographic in presidential elections. While traditionally aligned with the Democratic Party, Catholic voters have increasingly split their support between the two major parties in recent elections, reflecting the diversity of opinion within the church itself on issues such as abortion, immigration, and social justice.

Similarly, Jewish voters have historically supported Democratic candidates, but there has been significant attention paid to the Jewish vote in recent elections, especially as tensions over foreign policy issues—such as the U.S. relationship with Israel—have played a prominent role in shaping political discourse.

Religious identity has also become an important factor in the election of candidates. Candidates must increasingly address the concerns of religious voters, navigating a complex terrain of faith-based values, policy preferences, and social issues. Whether it is Donald Trump's focus on religious freedom, Joe Biden's support for Catholic social teachings, or Barack Obama's outreach to Black churches, candidates must continually engage with religious groups in order to win the support of their members.

The role of churches in American presidential elections is multifaceted and enduring. Religious institutions serve as critical platforms for voter mobilization, influence political ideologies, and play a crucial role in shaping the outcome of elections. From the rise of the Religious Right to the influence of African American churches and the evolving role of religious diversity, churches remain powerful actors in American political life.

As religion continues to play a central role in American society, its impact on presidential elections will only grow. The challenge for politicians and voters alike is to navigate the complexities of religion and politics, recognizing both the potential for divisiveness and the power of faith-based movements to bring about meaningful change. Ultimately, churches in America will continue to shape the political landscape, influencing presidential elections and guiding voters' choices for generations to come.

The Impact of Social Media on Elections

The rise of social media has fundamentally transformed the landscape of modern elections. What was once a political system driven primarily by traditional media such as television, radio, and newspapers, is now highly influenced by social platforms like Facebook, Twitter, Instagram, and more recently, TikTok. These platforms have become a central hub for political discourse, voter engagement, and campaign strategy. Social media is no longer just a tool for connecting people; it has become one of the most powerful forces in shaping public opinion, mobilizing voters, and even determining the outcomes of elections. This essay will explore the ways in which social media has impacted elections, including its role in voter engagement, political polarization, misinformation, campaign strategies, and its growing influence in both local and national elections.

1. Social Media as a Platform for Political Discourse

One of the most significant ways in which social media has influenced elections is by providing a space for political discourse that is decentralized and accessible. In the past, political dialogue in the U.S. was largely shaped by a few key media outlets that controlled the flow of information. However, with the advent of social media, the flow of political information is no longer in the hands of a few powerful organizations. Instead, ordinary citizens, politicians, political parties, and even foreign actors can now participate in public conversations, spread information, and mobilize supporters.

The Democratization of Information

Social media has democratized political communication by giving everyone with an internet connection a voice. This has allowed for a more diverse array of perspectives to be heard, especially among marginalized groups that previously had limited access to traditional media platforms. Activists, grassroots organizations, and social movements have been able to use social media to amplify their messages, organize protests, and promote policy changes. For instance, movements such as #BlackLivesMatter and #MeToo gained significant traction through social media platforms, which helped to elevate issues of racial justice and gender equality in the public consciousness. In terms of elections, candidates have been able to use social media to communicate directly with voters, bypassing traditional gatekeepers of information such as journalists and broadcasters.

However, the democratization of information has also led to challenges. While social media has given a voice to many, it has also created an environment where misinformation, disinformation, and extremism can thrive. The ease with which anyone can share content, whether true or false, has led to concerns over the spread of fake news and its potential impact on elections.

Public Debate and Political Polarization

Social media has also become a key space for public debate. Platforms like Twitter have allowed citizens to engage in real-time conversations about political events, policies, and elections. This has led to greater political awareness and engagement among many users, especially younger generations who may not have been as engaged in traditional political processes. Through hashtags, trending topics, and viral posts, social media users can drive national conversations and shape the public agenda.

At the same time, the way social media algorithms work has contributed to increasing political polarization. Social media platforms tend to show users content that aligns with their existing beliefs, creating "filter bubbles" where users are exposed only to information that confirms their preconceptions. This selective exposure has been linked to growing political polarization, as users become more entrenched in their ideological positions. During election periods, this dynamic is often heightened, with users engaging more in partisan discourse, sometimes at the expense of civil debate.

The polarization effect has been particularly pronounced in the United States, where social media has become a breeding ground for echo chambers, where people with similar political views reinforce each other's beliefs. This has contributed to the rise of political extremism, with social media platforms often acting as incubators for radical political ideas. As users share content that aligns with their views, it can lead to more extreme rhetoric, less willingness to compromise, and an increased sense of "us versus them."

2. Social Media and Voter Engagement

Social media platforms have transformed how political campaigns engage with voters, allowing for direct communication and real-time interaction. Unlike traditional methods of campaigning, such as television ads and rallies, social media allows candidates to connect with voters on a more personal level. This shift has altered how campaigns are conducted and has made voter engagement a central component of modern election strategy.

Targeted Campaigning and Micro-Targeting

One of the most powerful features of social media is its ability to enable micro-targeting—tailoring political messages to specific groups of voters based on their interests, behaviors, and demographics. Political campaigns can use data analytics to identify key voter segments and create personalized messages aimed at mobilizing these groups. Social media platforms, particularly Facebook, have allowed campaigns to gather vast amounts of data on users, which can then be used to send highly targeted ads and content to potential voters.

Micro-targeting is particularly effective in persuading undecided voters, motivating potential supporters, and driving voter turnout. The Obama campaigns in 2008 and 2012 were early pioneers in using social media for micro-targeting, particularly through Facebook ads. These campaigns used data analytics to identify voters who were likely to support Obama but needed an extra push to get to the polls. The success of these campaigns showed the potential of social media in electoral politics.

However, micro-targeting also raises significant concerns about privacy, data security, and the ethical implications of using personal data for political gain. The scandal surrounding Cambridge Analytica, in which data from millions of Facebook users was harvested to create targeted political ads for Donald Trump's 2016 presidential campaign, brought these issues to the forefront. Critics argue that the use of personal data in elections can be manipulative, undermining the democratic process by exploiting voters' private information without their consent.

Increased Political Participation Among Young Voters

Social media has had a particularly pronounced effect on youth engagement in elections. Younger voters, who are often less likely to engage with traditional media, are far more likely to consume political content on social media platforms. According to studies, young voters—particularly those between the ages of 18 and 34—are more likely to get their news from social media than from traditional news outlets. As a result, social media has become a key tool for political campaigns to reach and mobilize this demographic.

During the 2016 and 2020 U.S. presidential elections, social media played a key role in encouraging young people to vote. The viral spread of hashtags, memes, and videos promoting political participation was particularly effective in rallying younger voters around specific causes, such as climate change, racial justice, and healthcare reform. Social media has allowed young voters to connect with political movements, learn about the issues, and become active participants in the political process.

While social media has increased political participation among young voters, it has also been criticized for spreading shallow political content that may not adequately inform voters about important issues. Social media platforms are often designed for quick, bite-sized content, which can make it difficult for users to engage with complex political issues in a meaningful way. This can result in a form of "slacktivism," where individuals express political views online but fail to translate these views into tangible political actions, such as voting.

3. Misinformation, Disinformation, and Fake News

Perhaps one of the most controversial impacts of social media on elections is the spread of misinformation and disinformation. While social media platforms have the potential to foster informed political dialogue, they have also become breeding grounds for false and misleading content that can shape voters' perceptions and behavior.

The Spread of Misinformation and Disinformation

Misinformation refers to the inadvertent sharing of false information, while disinformation refers to the intentional spread of false or misleading content to deceive others. Both types of information can have significant consequences for the democratic process, especially during elections. Social media platforms, with their fast-paced and viral nature, provide an ideal environment for both misinformation and disinformation to spread quickly.

The 2016 U.S. presidential election highlighted the dangers of misinformation and disinformation in the age of social media. Fake news stories, such as those claiming that the Pope endorsed Donald Trump or that Hillary Clinton was involved in a child trafficking ring, spread widely on Facebook and Twitter. These false stories were often shared by millions of users, contributing to a climate of distrust and confusion among voters.

Disinformation campaigns are often orchestrated by foreign actors, who use social media platforms to interfere in elections and sow division. The Russian interference in the 2016 election, in which Russian operatives used social media to spread divisive content and manipulate public opinion, is one of the most high-profile examples of how foreign entities can exploit social media for political gain. This interference has raised concerns about the vulnerability of democratic elections to manipulation via social media, especially given the lack of regulation and oversight of these platforms.

Social media platforms have responded to these challenges by implementing fact-checking programs, removing fake accounts, and taking down misleading content. However, these efforts have been met with criticism, with some arguing that they are insufficient or that they infringe on free speech. The debate over how to address misinformation and disinformation on social media is ongoing, and it remains one of the most pressing issues in modern electoral politics.

Echo Chambers and Confirmation Bias

Social media algorithms tend to prioritize content that aligns with users' previous interactions and preferences, creating "echo chambers" in which people are exposed primarily to information that reinforces their existing beliefs. This can lead to confirmation bias, where individuals seek out and engage with content that confirms their opinions while ignoring contradictory information. Echo chambers can contribute to polarization, as people become more entrenched in their political positions and less willing to engage with opposing viewpoints.

During elections, echo chambers can have a particularly pronounced effect, as voters are often exposed to political content that supports their chosen candidate or party. This can make it more difficult for individuals to critically evaluate political information and make informed decisions. It also limits the opportunity for constructive dialogue across ideological divides, further deepening political polarization.

4. Social Media as a Tool for Campaign Strategy

Campaigns have increasingly embraced social media as a central tool for engaging with voters, fundraising, and organizing. Social media allows candidates to communicate directly with voters, promote their policies, and react in real-time to developments in the election. Candidates no longer need to rely solely on television or radio ads to reach the electorate; they can now interact directly with millions of people through platforms like Twitter and Facebook.

Real-Time Communication and Crisis Management

Social media allows political campaigns to engage in real-time communication, whether it's responding to breaking news, reacting to opponents' attacks, or promoting positive news about the candidate. During the 2016 and 2020 U.S. presidential elections, Twitter became a key platform for candidates to communicate with voters, as well as with the media and political pundits. Donald Trump, in particular, was known for his prolific use of Twitter, where he would make policy announcements, comment on the news, and respond to criticisms—all in an unfiltered manner.

While real-time communication can be beneficial, it can also be a double-edged sword. Social media platforms are highly reactive, and candidates must be able to manage the constant flow of information and address crises quickly. A poorly worded tweet or controversial post can easily go viral, leading to negative press coverage or a loss of voter support.

Fundraising and Mobilization

Social media has become an essential tool for fundraising in modern elections. Platforms like Facebook, Instagram, and Twitter allow candidates to reach large audiences and solicit small donations from a broad base of supporters. Online fundraising has become increasingly important in U.S. elections, especially for candidates running in primaries or in races where traditional fundraising channels are less accessible.

Social media platforms also enable campaigns to mobilize supporters by encouraging them to share content, organize events, and participate in grassroots activities. Social media can be used to coordinate volunteer efforts, promote rallies and events, and increase voter turnout.

Impact

Social media has had a profound impact on elections in the United States and around the world. It has revolutionized the way campaigns engage with voters, reshaped political discourse, and contributed to both positive and negative aspects of the democratic process. Social media has made it easier for political campaigns to reach a wider audience, mobilize supporters, and encourage voter participation. At the same time, it has contributed to political polarization, the spread of misinformation, and the manipulation of voters by foreign actors.

As social media continues to evolve, it will undoubtedly play an increasingly central role in elections, both in the U.S. and globally. The challenge for political campaigns, voters, and policymakers will be to navigate the complexities of social media and harness its potential while addressing its risks. The future of social media in elections will depend on how these challenges are managed, and how effectively society can strike a balance between free expression and the integrity of the democratic process.

The Impact of Russia on American Elections

The impact of Russia on American elections has been one of the most significant and contentious issues in recent political history. Russia's interference in the 2016 U.S. presidential election, and its continued influence in subsequent elections, has raised serious questions about the integrity of democratic processes, the role of foreign actors in elections, and the growing use of technology to manipulate public opinion. This essay will examine the methods Russia has used to influence American elections, the scope and scale of its activities, the implications for U.S. democracy, and the ongoing debates surrounding foreign interference and its consequences.

1. Historical Context: Russia and U.S. Relations

To understand the nature of Russia's interference in American elections, it is important to first consider the broader historical context of U.S.-Russia relations. Throughout much of the 20th century, the United States and the Soviet Union were locked in a geopolitical struggle for global dominance, with the Cold War representing the peak of this rivalry. While the collapse of the Soviet Union in 1991 led to a temporary thaw in relations, tensions between the U.S. and Russia have remained high due to a variety of issues, including the expansion of NATO, U.S. foreign interventions, and disputes over international norms and governance.

Under President Vladimir Putin, who has been in power in Russia for over two decades, Russia has sought to reassert its influence on the global stage, including challenging the United States politically, economically, and militarily. Putin's government has been accused of using a range of tactics to undermine Western democracies, including cyberattacks, disinformation campaigns, and support for authoritarian leaders who share Russia's anti-Western sentiments.

The 2016 U.S. presidential election marked a turning point in this rivalry, with Russian interference reaching a new level of sophistication and scale. The allegations of Russian involvement in the election raised significant concerns about the vulnerability of the American democratic process to foreign influence.

2. The 2016 Election: Russian Interference and Its Methods

The 2016 U.S. presidential election was the first to face a coordinated and sustained campaign of interference by Russia. Intelligence agencies, including the CIA and the FBI, have since confirmed that the Russian government, at the behest of President Putin, sought to interfere in the election to benefit the candidacy of Donald Trump and undermine the campaign of Hillary Clinton. There is significant evidence to prove the same was true concerning the campaign of Kamala Harris. Russia's methods were multifaceted and involved a range of tactics designed to manipulate public opinion, sow division, and disrupt the electoral process.

Hack-and-Leak Operations: The DNC Email Scandal

One of the most high-profile elements of Russia's interference in the 2016 election was the hack-and-leak operation targeting the Democratic National Committee (DNC). In 2016, Russian hackers, believed to be working for Russia's GRU (military intelligence agency), infiltrated the DNC's email system and obtained thousands of private emails, which were then released to the public through platforms like WikiLeaks. These emails revealed sensitive and embarrassing information about the DNC's handling of the Democratic primaries, including evidence that the party had favored Hillary Clinton over Bernie Sanders, and sparked a political firestorm.

The release of the emails was timed to coincide with key moments in the election cycle, such as the Democratic National Convention, and aimed to damage the reputation of Clinton and the Democratic Party. The leak fed into broader narratives of corruption and elitism, undermining public trust in Clinton's campaign and the political establishment.

The hack-and-leak operation was widely seen as an attempt by Russia to create division within the U.S. political system and undermine the credibility of Clinton, whom Putin reportedly viewed as a political adversary due to her hawkish stance on Russia and support for the 2011 Russian protests. By releasing damaging information at strategic points, Russia sought to fuel controversy and undermine public confidence in the election's fairness.

Disinformation Campaigns and Social Media Manipulation

In addition to hacking and leaking emails, Russia also launched a vast disinformation campaign on social media platforms like Facebook, Twitter, and Instagram. Russia's Internet Research Agency (IRA), a St. Petersburg-based troll farm with close ties to the Russian government, played a central role in this effort. The IRA created fake social media accounts designed to resemble real American citizens, which were used to spread divisive political content, amplify false narratives, and manipulate public opinion.

The disinformation campaigns targeted key issues such as race relations, immigration, gun control, and the legitimacy of the electoral process. For example, IRA operatives used social media to exacerbate racial tensions by organizing rallies and protests for both pro- and anti-Black Lives Matter causes, fostering division among American communities. Additionally, Russian operatives created misleading ads and posts that sought to undermine the credibility of Clinton's candidacy while promoting Trump's campaign. These ads often used hyperbolic or false statements to stoke fear and distrust.

Russian operatives also targeted specific demographic groups, including African Americans, Latinos, and millennials. By exploiting the deep political divisions in the U.S. and capitalizing on social issues such as racial inequality and economic frustration, Russia sought to sow division and reduce voter turnout for Clinton. In particular, Russian-backed social media accounts promoted messages that discouraged African Americans from voting, urging them to abstain from the election or vote for third-party candidates.

Hacking of State Election Systems

Another significant element of Russia's interference in the 2016 election was its attempt to infiltrate state election systems. Russian hackers targeted the voter registration databases and election infrastructure of several states, including Illinois and Arizona, with the goal of disrupting the voting process or influencing the results. While there was no evidence that any votes were altered or deleted, the intrusion into election systems raised serious concerns about the security of U.S. electoral infrastructure.

These efforts to breach election systems were part of a broader Russian strategy to undermine confidence in the U.S. electoral process and sow doubts about the legitimacy of the election outcome. By targeting election systems, Russia aimed to create a perception of chaos and insecurity, which could erode public trust in the election results and potentially delegitimize the outcome.

Russian Support for Trump and Disruption of Clinton's Campaign

The broader goal of Russia's interference in the 2016 election was to help elect Donald Trump and undermine Hillary Clinton's candidacy. Trump's rhetoric, particularly his criticism of NATO, his admiration for Putin, and his isolationist foreign policy stance, was seen as aligning with Russia's strategic interests. By supporting Trump, Russia sought to destabilize Western alliances, reduce U.S. influence in global affairs, and undermine democratic norms.

Trump's campaign, in turn, benefited from Russia's disinformation efforts, which targeted Clinton's weaknesses and amplified Trump's messages. Russian-backed social media posts, fake news stories, and hacked emails were designed to discredit Clinton, portraying her as corrupt and untrustworthy. These efforts were particularly effective in key battleground states, where they may have swayed the votes of undecided or disillusioned voters.

In addition to its digital interference, Russia also reportedly made efforts to establish contacts with the Trump campaign, including through intermediaries like Paul Manafort, the campaign's former chairman, who had ties to pro-Russian politicians in Ukraine. The Trump campaign's connections with Russia, though extensively investigated, have been the subject of ongoing debate, with some critics claiming that Trump and his associates may have been complicit in Russia's interference, while others argue that there was insufficient evidence of direct coordination.

3. The Mueller Investigation and Legal Findings

In response to the allegations of Russian interference, Special Counsel Robert Mueller was appointed to investigate the scope of Russia's involvement in the 2016 election. The Mueller Report, published in 2019, confirmed that Russia had interfered in the election, but did not find conclusive evidence that the Trump campaign had coordinated directly with Russia. The report outlined the various ways in which Russia had attempted to influence the election, including the hacking of emails, disinformation campaigns, and cyberattacks on state election systems.

While Mueller's investigation did not find criminal conspiracy between Trump's campaign and Russia, it did highlight numerous contacts between Trump's associates and Russian operatives, some of which were suspicious but did not meet the legal standard for charges of collusion. The report also identified efforts by the Trump campaign to obstruct the investigation, though Mueller refrained from making a determination on whether obstruction of justice occurred, leaving that decision to Congress.

Despite the report's conclusions, the investigation and its findings further fueled political polarization in the U.S., with some members of Congress and the public calling for greater accountability for both Russia's interference and the Trump campaign's conduct. The Mueller investigation, censored and released after being falsely and publicly discredited by the Trump administration, did not quell the broader concerns about foreign interference in U.S. elections.

4. Russian Influence in Subsequent Elections

Although the 2016 election was the most high-profile instance of Russian interference, there have been ongoing concerns about Russia's efforts to influence subsequent elections. In the 2020 U.S. presidential election, Russian operatives were again accused of engaging in disinformation campaigns to sow division and undermine the legitimacy of the election process. While there were no reports of widespread interference in voting or vote tallying, Russia's social media campaigns continued, targeting American political polarization and amplifying extremist content.

In addition to social media manipulation, Russian intelligence agencies have been accused of spreading misinformation about the integrity of the 2020 election, with the goal of undermining confidence in the democratic process and fostering distrust in the legitimacy of the election results. These efforts were compounded by domestic actors who falsely claimed that the election was "stolen" from Donald Trump, leading to the storming of the U.S. Capitol on January 6, 2021.

Russia's continued involvement in American politics has raised concerns about the vulnerability of U.S. elections to foreign interference, particularly in light of advancements in cyber technology and social media manipulation. The U.S. government has responded to these threats by increasing its efforts to secure election infrastructure, improving cybersecurity, and raising awareness about the risks of disinformation campaigns. However, the threat of foreign influence remains a significant concern for future elections.

5. The Broader Implications for U.S. Democracy

The impact of Russian interference in U.S. elections has had profound implications for American democracy. Foreign meddling in elections undermines the foundational principle of democratic self-determination, where the will of the people should be the determining factor in political outcomes. Russia's efforts to manipulate public opinion, sow division, and influence election results have highlighted the vulnerabilities in the U.S. electoral system, particularly in the age of social media and digital communication.

Beyond the immediate effects on election outcomes, Russian interference has deepened political polarization in the U.S., contributing to a climate of mistrust and division. By amplifying existing political and social fractures, Russia has succeeded in making Americans more distrustful of their institutions and each other. This undermines the social cohesion necessary for the functioning of a healthy democracy and presents long-term challenges for the integrity of U.S. elections.

Furthermore, Russia's interference has raised broader questions about the regulation of social media platforms, the role of foreign actors in shaping domestic political discourse, and the need for increased transparency and accountability in the digital age. The U.S. government has taken steps to address these issues, but the fight against foreign interference is ongoing and requires a coordinated effort from government agencies, tech companies, and civil society organizations.

Russia Continues to Interfere

Russia's interference in American elections has been one of the most significant challenges to U.S. democracy in the modern era. Through cyberattacks, disinformation campaigns, and attempts to influence political outcomes, Russia seeks to destabilize the American political system and undermine public trust in democratic institutions. While the extent of Russia's direct involvement in influencing the 2016 and 2024 elections remains a subject of debate, its impact on the political landscape has been profound and lasting.

The lessons from Russia's interference underscore the need for greater vigilance, cybersecurity, and accountability in the digital age. As technology continues to evolve, so too will the methods of foreign actors seeking to manipulate elections. The future of American democracy depends on the ability to safeguard the electoral process from external threats and to foster a more informed and resilient electorate.

The Impact of Israel and Gaza on the 2024 U.S. Presidential Election

The relationship between the United States and Israel, as well as the ongoing conflict between Israel and Gaza, has long been a sensitive and influential issue in American politics. These issues often come to the forefront during presidential elections, as candidates navigate complex foreign policy positions, appeal to domestic political constituencies, and try to balance the interests of various influential groups within the U.S. electorate. The dynamics surrounding Israel and Gaza are not only significant in terms of U.S. foreign policy, but they also have profound implications for domestic politics, shaping debates over national security, humanitarian concerns, and the broader geopolitical landscape. It is crucial to understand how these issues could influence the candidates, their platforms, and the voters who care deeply about the Middle East conflict.

1. Israel and Gaza: A Longstanding U.S. Foreign Policy Issue

The United States has had a long-standing relationship with Israel, dating back to the establishment of the state of Israel in 1948. U.S. support for Israel has been consistent over the decades, driven by a combination of shared democratic values, strategic interests in the Middle East, and political pressures from key domestic constituencies, particularly Jewish-American voters and evangelical Christians. However, this support has often been a source of tension, both domestically and internationally.

The conflict between Israel and Gaza, and more broadly between Israel and the Palestinian territories, has been one of the central issues in Middle Eastern geopolitics for over a century. The Gaza Strip, a densely populated region along the Mediterranean Sea, is home to a large Palestinian population, many of whom are displaced refugees from the 1948 Arab-Israeli War. The territory is governed by Hamas, an Islamist militant organization that has been in power since 2007 and which has been involved in repeated clashes with Israel over issues ranging from territory to religious control of holy sites.

The political complexities of the Israel-Gaza conflict play out on the global stage, including in U.S. elections. In particular, American presidents have often been put in a position where they must balance strong support for Israel with a growing recognition of the humanitarian situation in Gaza and the wider Palestinian territories. As the violence between Israel and Gaza flares up periodically, it reverberates throughout American politics, influencing voters, particularly those who are closely aligned with the Palestinian cause, Jewish-American groups, and evangelical Christians, each of whom bring their own set of priorities to the table.

2. Impact of Israel and Gaza on U.S. Politics

Jewish-American Voters

Jewish-American voters have long been a key demographic in U.S. elections, and their views on Israel and the Gaza conflict significantly impact political discourse, especially within the context of presidential elections. Historically, Jewish voters in the U.S. have overwhelmingly supported the Democratic Party, but their views on Israel and the Middle East have sometimes led to divisions within the party, particularly as the political situation in Gaza has intensified.

While many Jewish-Americans strongly support Israel, there is also a growing segment of the Jewish community in the U.S. that is critical of Israel's policies toward the Palestinians, particularly with regard to the humanitarian situation in Gaza. Progressive Jewish groups, such as J Street, have increasingly called for a more balanced approach to the Israeli-Palestinian conflict, advocating for a two-state solution and expressing concern over the treatment of Palestinians under Israeli occupation.

The tension between maintaining strong ties to Israel while addressing human rights concerns in Gaza has presented a challenge for U.S. politicians, particularly those seeking to appeal to Jewish-American voters. In the 2020 election, for instance, the Democratic Party found itself divided over how to address Israel's policies, with some candidates advocating for a more critical stance toward Israel, while others, including former President Joe Biden, continued to express unwavering support for Israel's right to defend itself. This division played an important role in the 2024 election

Evangelical Christians and Pro-Israel Lobbying

Evangelical Christians in the United States, who make up a significant portion of the Republican base, are among the most ardent supporters of Israel. Many evangelical Christians view Israel as central to their religious beliefs, particularly in relation to the biblical significance of the Holy Land and the belief in the Second Coming of Christ. This theological support for Israel often translates into strong political backing, and evangelical voters are typically unwavering in their commitment to Israel's security.

The evangelical community's support for Israel has been a key factor in shaping U.S. foreign policy over the years, with candidates often adopting pro-Israel stances to appeal to this influential voting bloc. In 2017, President Donald Trump's decision to move the U.S. embassy in Israel from Tel Aviv to Jerusalem was a highly symbolic act that resonated deeply with evangelical voters and further cemented their support for his administration. This move was seen as fulfilling a longstanding evangelical desire to recognize Jerusalem as the capital of

Israel, and it was hailed as a victory for both Trump and the evangelical community.

Evangelical support for Israel will continue to be a significant factor in elections. Republican candidates emphasize their pro-Israel positions, both to maintain the support of this key constituency and to appeal to conservative Jewish voters who prioritize Israel's security. However, the growing recognition of Palestinian rights and the humanitarian situation in Gaza may create tensions, particularly if candidates are forced to balance these concerns with their pro-Israel stances.

The Progressive Left and Growing Criticism of Israeli Policy

On the progressive side of the political spectrum, especially within the Democratic Party, there has been increasing criticism of Israel's treatment of Palestinians, particularly in Gaza. Progressive activists, many of whom are young voters, have become more vocal in advocating for Palestinian rights and condemning Israel's military actions against Gaza. The recent escalations in Gaza, such as the 2021 conflict between Israel and Hamas, saw widespread protests and calls for the U.S. to reconsider its unwavering support for Israel, with some activists even advocating for policies such as cutting U.S. military aid to Israel or imposing sanctions in response to human rights abuses.

The Democratic Party has faced pressure from this growing left-wing movement to adopt a more balanced approach to the Israeli-Palestinian conflict. The party's progressive wing, led by figures such as Congresswoman Ilhan Omar, Senator Bernie Sanders, and Representative Alexandria Ocasio-Cortez, has pushed for a reexamination of U.S. policy toward Israel, particularly with regard to its treatment of Palestinians in Gaza and the West Bank. The debate over Israel and Gaza played a central role in shaping the 2024 election.

At the same time, the Democratic establishment, including President Joe Biden, has generally maintained a pro-Israel stance, emphasizing Israel's right to defend itself from attacks by Hamas and other militant groups. Biden has also expressed concern over the humanitarian situation in Gaza and has called for a two-state solution to resolve the conflict.

3. Geopolitical Implications of the Israel-Gaza Conflict on U.S. Elections

The Israel-Gaza conflict has significant geopolitical ramifications, and future leaders will need to navigate the broader Middle East dynamics as they develop their foreign policy platforms. The ongoing conflict between Israel and Hamas, and the broader Palestinian question, is just one piece of a complex puzzle that includes U.S. relations with Iran, Syria, Lebanon, and other regional powers.

U.S. Relations with Iran

The U.S. relationship with Iran is another factor that played into the 2024 election. Iran is a major supporter of Hamas and other militant groups in Gaza, and its role in the broader Middle East conflict, particularly with regard to its nuclear program, is a key concern for Israel. Leadership will be asked to address how they plan to handle Iran's regional influence, especially in relation to its support for militant groups in Gaza and its nuclear ambitions.

The U.S. reentry into the Iran nuclear deal (Joint Comprehensive Plan of Action, JCPOA), which was a significant campaign promise by President Biden in 2020, could have ramifications for Israel and Gaza. Israel strongly opposed the Iran deal, citing concerns about Iran's regional ambitions and its support for anti-Israel groups. If Biden or another Democratic candidate seeks to revive or renegotiate the JCPOA, it may create tensions with Israel, particularly if the agreement is perceived as weakening Israel's security. On the other hand, Republicans will likely emphasize a tougher stance on Iran and will use the issue of Israel's security to differentiate themselves from the Democrats.

The Arab-Israeli Peace Process

The Abraham Accords, brokered by the Trump administration in 2020, led to normalization agreements between Israel and several Arab nations, including the United Arab Emirates (UAE), Bahrain, Sudan, and Morocco. These agreements marked a significant shift in the region, as many Arab states previously refused to normalize relations with Israel until the Palestinian issue was resolved.

The 2024 election featured discussions about how the U.S. should approach the Arab-Israeli peace process moving forward. While some candidates touted the success of the Abraham Accords as a model for further peace agreements, others argued that a lasting solution to the Israeli-Palestinian conflict must be achieved before further normalization can take place. The fate of Gaza and the broader Palestinian issue will continue to shape the debate about how to achieve lasting peace in the region.

Israel and Gaza in the 2024 U.S. Presidential Election

The impact of Israel and Gaza on the 2024 U.S. presidential election was profound, as candidates navigated a complex web of domestic political considerations, foreign policy priorities, and regional dynamics. The U.S. relationship with Israel remains one of the most important and contentious issues in American politics, with significant implications for both domestic voters and international diplomacy. Candidates largely refused to address the humanitarian situation in Gaza, while responding to the growing influence of progressive voices calling for a more critical stance on Israeli policies.

As the situation in Gaza continues to evolve and tensions in the Middle East remain high, the debate over U.S. policy toward Israel and Palestine will undoubtedly be a key issue in the future. Whether through diplomatic efforts, foreign aid, or military support, the U.S. president will play a crucial role in shaping the future of the region.

The Role of Billionaires in the 2024 U.S. Presidential Election

The influence of billionaires on American politics has been a subject of intense debate for decades. Their role continues to be a topic of scrutiny, as wealthy individuals and their financial power significantly shape political campaigns, public policy, and electoral outcomes. Billionaires have long wielded considerable influence, particularly through political donations, media ownership, and advocacy efforts. This influence is amplified in an era of increasing wealth inequality and diminishing trust in democratic institutions.

Billionaires impact is immense in U.S. elections, including their role in campaign finance, the creation of Super PACs, their influence on political discourse through media ownership, and their involvement in funding political organizations and lobbying efforts. The 2024 election was influenced by the financial power of these individuals and their ability to shape political outcomes at the national and local levels.

1. Billionaire Influence on Campaign Finance

The Role of Political Donations

Billionaires have a profound effect on the financing of political campaigns, with their significant financial contributions playing a critical role in shaping the political landscape. U.S. election laws allow individuals to contribute substantial sums of money to political candidates, parties, and causes, and billionaires have historically used this opportunity to exercise influence over elections. Political donations from wealthy individuals provide candidates with the resources to run extensive advertising campaigns, conduct outreach efforts, and organize voter mobilization drives. These contributions, while often justified as a way to support democratic engagement, have led to concerns about the disproportionate influence of the rich over political processes.

One key turning point in the influence of billionaires on campaign finance came with the U.S. Supreme Court's landmark decision in *Citizens United v. Federal Election Commission* (2010). This ruling struck down restrictions on independent political spending, allowing corporations, unions, and individuals to spend unlimited amounts of money in support of political candidates or issues, as long as the spending was not directly coordinated with a campaign. As a result, billionaires and their allies were able to pour vast sums of money into the electoral process, potentially swaying elections in their favor.

For instance, in the 2020 election, several billionaires made significant contributions to Super PACs supporting presidential candidates and congressional races. Michael Bloomberg, the former New York City mayor and media mogul, spent over $1 billion of his personal wealth in his failed bid for the Democratic nomination. Meanwhile, figures like Sheldon Adelson (a major GOP donor) and Tom Steyer (a Democratic donor) also contributed tens of millions of dollars to political causes and candidates. These large sums of money are often funneled through Super PACs, which are able to influence elections by running ads, organizing campaigns, and supporting political messages.

The Creation of Super PACs and Dark Money

Super Political Action Committees (Super PACs) are entities that can accept unlimited contributions from individuals, corporations, and unions to advocate for or against political candidates. While Super PACs are not allowed to coordinate directly with a campaign, they have the ability to influence elections through their financial clout. Billionaires are often behind these Super PACs, using their wealth to promote candidates who align with their interests or to attack candidates they oppose. The Super PACs run ads, distribute campaign materials, and engage in grassroots lobbying efforts, all of which can sway public opinion.

Super PACs have become one of the most powerful mechanisms for billionaire influence in U.S. elections. According to reports, in the 2020 election cycle, roughly 60% of all spending in the presidential race came from Super PACs and outside groups, much of it funded by billionaires. The 2024 election saw even more spending through these channels, as billionaires used their wealth to shape the outcomes of key races.

Alongside Super PACs, a related issue is the role of "dark money" in U.S. elections. Dark money refers to political spending by nonprofit organizations that are not required to disclose their donors. These groups can raise and spend unlimited amounts of money to influence elections, and the donors behind these organizations are often hidden from the public. Many of these organizations, such as 501(c)(4) groups, are funded by wealthy individuals or corporations, allowing billionaires to influence elections without revealing their identities. Dark money has been a growing concern in U.S. politics, as it enables billionaires to anonymously pour large sums of money into races, further increasing their influence over political outcomes.

2. Billionaires and Media Ownership

Another significant way in which billionaires influence U.S. elections is through media ownership. Many of the most influential news outlets and media platforms are owned by a small number of wealthy individuals and corporations. These billionaires have the power to shape public discourse, determine which issues are covered, and influence the framing of political events. In this era of hyper-polarization and misinformation, media ownership has become an increasingly important lever of power.

For example, Rupert Murdoch, the media mogul behind Fox News and a number of other influential media properties, has long been a key player in shaping conservative political discourse in the U.S. Murdoch's media empire has played a crucial role in promoting conservative candidates and policies, particularly during presidential election cycles. Murdoch's influence was especially evident in the 2016 election, where Fox News played a pivotal role in elevating Donald Trump's candidacy and shaping public perceptions of his political opponents.

Similarly, other billionaires, such as Jeff Bezos (owner of The Washington Post) and Larry Page and Sergey Brin (co-founders of Google, which owns YouTube), wield significant influence over the dissemination of information to American voters. While these individuals may not directly control political messaging in the same way as Murdoch, their media platforms are integral to the way voters receive news, engage with political content, and form opinions. The algorithms of platforms like Google, YouTube, and Facebook have also been shown to amplify politically charged content, which can influence voter behavior, shape election outcomes, and contribute to political polarization.

Billionaires who own media outlets also have the ability to shape the narrative around key political issues. By selecting which stories to highlight, framing political events in a particular way, and deciding which candidates to promote or criticize, media moguls can influence public opinion and sway voters in critical elections. In the 2024 election, media moguls played an even greater role in shaping political discourse, particularly as digital and social media platforms became increasingly important for reaching voters.

3. Billionaires as Political Donors and Advocacy Groups

Beyond directly funding political campaigns, many billionaires exert influence over elections through their support for advocacy groups, think tanks, and other organizations that shape public policy and electoral outcomes. These advocacy groups often promote specific political ideologies, advance legislative agendas, and mobilize voters to support certain candidates or causes.

Billionaires like George Soros, who has been a prominent supporter of liberal causes and candidates, have established powerful networks of advocacy organizations that promote progressive policy goals. Soros, through his Open Society Foundations, has spent billions of dollars on initiatives aimed at advancing democracy, human rights, and criminal justice reform. Similarly, conservative billionaires like the Koch brothers have created powerful advocacy organizations, such as Americans for Prosperity, that promote free-market principles and conservative policies.

These advocacy organizations can play a key role in influencing the outcomes of elections by funding issue-based campaigns, engaging in voter outreach, and supporting candidates who align with their ideological goals. For instance, in the 2020 election, billionaires like Soros and the Koch network spent millions on ads supporting candidates and causes related to criminal justice reform, healthcare, and climate change.

In the 2024 election, these advocacy groups played a crucial role in shaping electoral outcomes. Wealthy individuals used their resources to fund grassroots efforts, mobilize voters, and push for policies that align with their interests. Whether it is through promoting climate action, advancing healthcare reform, or supporting criminal justice reform, billionaires will continue to leverage their wealth to influence the political agenda in the lead-up to elections.

4. The Growing Power of Big Tech and Billionaire Influence

In addition to traditional forms of media ownership and political donations, the growing power of big tech companies represents a new frontier for billionaire influence on U.S. elections. Companies like Facebook, Twitter, and Google, which are owned by some of the world's wealthiest individuals, have become central players in the political arena, particularly as social media and digital platforms increasingly shape public discourse.

Billionaires like Mark Zuckerberg (Facebook) and Jack Dorsey (Twitter) have faced growing scrutiny over their platforms' role in spreading misinformation, promoting political polarization, and shaping electoral outcomes. In the 2020 election, for example, Facebook played a central role in the spread of disinformation and conspiracy theories, with many critics accusing the platform of allowing false information to proliferate. Meanwhile, Twitter has become a key battleground for political discourse, with politicians, activists, and voters using the platform to share ideas, rally support, and engage with candidates.

The power of these tech platforms, and the billionaires behind them, has raised concerns about the fairness of U.S. elections. Social media algorithms that amplify certain political messages can create echo chambers, where voters are exposed only to content that aligns with their pre existing views. This can contribute to the spread of misinformation and exacerbate political polarization, making it harder for voters to make informed decisions.

The role of big tech and its billionaire owners in shaping political discourse will only grow in importance. Whether through targeted political ads, social media campaigns, or the amplification of certain narratives, the financial power of these tech moguls will be an important factor in elections.

The Growing Influence of Billionaires in U.S. Elections

Billionaires have become an increasingly powerful force in U.S. elections, shaping political discourse, funding campaigns, and influencing public policy. Through their political donations, ownership of media outlets, and support for advocacy groups, billionaires have the resources to shape the political landscape and influence the outcome of elections. Billionaires role in American politics will likely continue to grow, raising important questions about the fairness and integrity of the democratic process.

The influence of billionaires in U.S. elections underscores the growing problem of wealth inequality in American society, where a small group of individuals have the ability to wield disproportionate power over political outcomes. Whether through Super PACs, media ownership, or advocacy groups, the financial power of billionaires has the potential to shape electoral outcomes in ways that reflect their own interests, rather than those of the broader electorate.

After the 2024 election, it is essential for voters, policymakers, and advocacy groups to consider the impact of billionaire influence on the democratic process. Ensuring that elections remain fair, transparent, and representative of the will of the people requires addressing the growing concentration of political power in the hands of a few wealthy individuals. The future of American democracy depends on finding ways to limit the outsized influence of billionaires and ensure that the voices of everyday citizens are heard in the political arena.

The Impact of World War II Research on Politics

The idea of WWII's psychological research influencing American elections is not a widely known or direct subject in historical discourse. However, if we interpret this question as asking about how psychological tactics associated with propaganda, mass manipulation, or the broader field of psychological warfare might have influenced American political campaigns, there is a much richer historical discussion to be had.

Adolf Hitler's regime, underpinned by psychological manipulation, mass propaganda, and the ability to shape public perception, has influenced political communication and the study of psychological operations (PsyOps), though its direct relevance to modern American elections is more indirect.

We can, however, explore the impact of propaganda, psychological tactics, and mass manipulation techniques that were employed by Hitler's regime, and how these ideas have evolved and influenced political campaigns in the U.S., including election strategies, messaging, and voter behavior manipulation. Here's a framework for how such tactics may still be relevant:

1. The Origins of Psychological Warfare and Propaganda

The use of psychological research and propaganda during Adolf Hitler's rule became one of the most studied aspects of totalitarian control. The Nazis utilized mass propaganda to control the public narrative and gain mass support, and psychologists such as Joseph Goebbels, the Nazi Minister of Propaganda, understood the power of mass psychology. Goebbels, in particular, was a master at using the media to manipulate public opinion and create a highly controlled narrative.

In many ways, the use of propaganda in Nazi Germany laid the foundation for understanding how psychological manipulation could be applied on a large scale. The understanding of group dynamics, emotional appeals, and the strategic use of media for political purposes was advanced significantly during this time.

These methods, while deeply troubling in their historical context, laid the groundwork for subsequent developments in political communication, marketing, and voter psychology.

2. Psychological Insights in American Politics

In the aftermath of World War II, many of the psychological principles that the Nazis applied to propaganda were absorbed into U.S. military and political strategies. The U.S. government and private entities have long studied how to sway public opinion using the principles of persuasion, perception management, and group psychology. These studies were particularly relevant during the Cold War, where controlling public opinion was seen as key to ideological battles against the Soviet Union.

As the U.S. entered the media age and began to embrace television as a primary method of communication in the 1950s, these insights into psychological manipulation of public perception became crucial for political campaigns. Political scientists and campaign strategists realized that they could shape voter behavior through careful message crafting, framing, and targeting key emotional appeals.

Key Examples of Psychological Tactics in American Elections:

1. **Television Debates and Image Politics**: The first televised presidential debates between Richard Nixon and John F. Kennedy in 1960 were a pivotal moment in American politics. Kennedy's polished appearance, while Nixon appeared sweaty and uncomfortable, highlighted the importance of perception and the psychological impact of

television on voters. The physical image, body language, and personal appeal became central to winning elections.

1. **Nixon's "Southern Strategy"**: Richard Nixon used psychological appeals to the fear of racial change and the emotional response to civil rights movements. By appealing to white Southerners' anxieties and feelings of cultural displacement, Nixon's campaign successfully capitalized on emotional rhetoric to win over voters who felt disconnected from the political establishment's shift toward racial equality.

1. **The "War on Drugs"**: Ronald Reagan's administration used psychological appeals to fear, associating crime and social unrest with drug use. This appeal to fear (as well as the demonization of minorities and the stigmatization of drugs) proved effective in rallying a political base that felt under siege.

3. The Psychological Influence of Media and Campaign Advertising

One of the most significant legacies of the psychological insights gained from Nazi-era propaganda was the understanding that media could be used to craft perceptions and shape emotions. Campaign advertising in the U.S. has long relied on these psychological tactics.

Adolf Hitler's use of symbols, emotional messaging, and scapegoating through propaganda was studied after the war. His manipulation of public opinion through the use of emotionally charged messages and symbols is still relevant today. Campaigns often rely on fear, anger, and hope—emotions that have their roots in psychological research that, in some cases, could be traced back to early 20th-century propaganda techniques.

Examples of Media Psychology in American Campaigns:

1. **The "Daisy" Ad (1964)**: Lyndon B. Johnson's campaign released a famous ad known as the "Daisy" ad, which was designed to evoke fear about the possibility of nuclear war under Barry Goldwater's leadership. The ad showed a young girl counting petals on a daisy, followed by an explosion, while a voiceover warned of the dangers of Goldwater's policies. This was a classic use of fear tactics to sway voters emotionally.

1. **Negative Campaigning**: Negative ads, which have become a staple of modern American politics, rely heavily on the psychological principle of association. By associating an opponent with negative emotions—such as dishonesty, corruption, or weakness—campaigns seek to weaken the opponent's image. These techniques are rooted in psychological theories of aversion and how negative stimuli can outweigh positive impressions.

1. **Microtargeting and Big Data**: In the age of digital media, the psychological manipulation of voters has entered a new frontier. Through social media platforms and sophisticated data analytics, campaigns can now tailor specific messages to individual voters based on their behavior, preferences, and emotional responses. The use of "big data" allows campaigns to apply psychological insights with unprecedented precision, ensuring that the most effective messages reach the most receptive audiences.

4. The Legacy of Psychological Tactics in Modern Campaigns

The psychological principles behind propaganda are still embedded in modern political campaigns. Campaign managers, political consultants, and media strategists utilize these tools to sway public opinion, mobilize supporters, and create favorable narratives about their candidates. These tools—rooted in the psychological manipulation of mass sentiment—are vital components of electoral strategy.

Some of the key psychological elements that persist in American elections today include:

1. **Framing**: The way issues are framed can drastically alter the public's perception. For example, a policy may be framed as "tax relief" versus "tax cuts for the wealthy." These subtle shifts in language trigger different emotional responses, appealing to the values of different voter segments.

1. **Fear and Anger**: Much like Goebbels' use of fear and anger to rally support for the Nazi regime, U.S. political campaigns have been known to stoke fear about immigration, crime, terrorism, or economic collapse. Fear is a powerful motivator in political campaigns, and it is often used to persuade voters to support candidates who promise security or protection.

1. **Hope and Identity Politics**: Positive emotions, such as hope and pride, are just as critical in modern campaigns. Barack Obama's 2008 campaign famously capitalized on the idea of hope and change, using a hopeful narrative to inspire voters. In contrast, Donald Trump's 2016 campaign used a strong appeal to identity, focusing on American nationalism and framing issues such as immigration as a threat to national identity.

1. **Cognitive Biases**: Understanding how people make decisions based on cognitive biases—such as confirmation bias or the anchoring effect—has become a key part of

modern political strategy. These biases influence how voters process information and make decisions, and campaigns take advantage of them to shape perceptions and increase their chances of victory.

5. The Ethical Considerations: Psychological Manipulation vs. Democratic Integrity

While psychological tactics can undoubtedly influence election outcomes, they also raise ethical concerns. The manipulation of public opinion through emotional appeals, misinformation, and psychological warfare undermines the democratic process by prioritizing persuasion over informed decision-making. The use of fear, disinformation, and division can erode trust in political institutions and lead to a more polarized electorate.

The use of psychological research in elections thus forces a reckoning with questions about the ethical boundaries of persuasion. Are politicians and campaigns crossing a line when they exploit fear or anger to win votes? Should the use of data and microtargeting be regulated to ensure fairer elections? These are questions that are becoming more pressing as election strategies evolve and psychological techniques become increasingly sophisticated.

Hitler's Psychological Influence—Indirect, but Enduring

While Adolf Hitler's direct psychological research may not be a primary influence in American elections, the psychological tactics used during his regime—especially in propaganda and mass mobilization—have indirectly shaped modern political strategies. From the use of fear to the careful crafting of narratives, political campaigns today still draw on the principles of emotional persuasion, cognitive biases, and mass media influence that were central to Nazi propaganda efforts.

As American elections increasingly rely on digital media, social media, and microtargeting, the psychological manipulation of voters is only becoming more pervasive and powerful. The legacy of psychological research on mass manipulation, while born from darker times, is a crucial element of the strategies that guide political campaigns today.

In the 2024 elections, the psychological principles rooted in these earlier forms of propaganda shaped political discourse. The challenge for American democracy is to ensure that these tactics are not used to undermine the integrity of the electoral process or deepen the divides within society, but instead foster a political environment in which voters are empowered to make informed and thoughtful decisions.

The fear of political collapse, whether from internal strife, external conflict, or societal upheaval, has periodically cast a long shadow over the world throughout history. These moments of uncertainty often emerge during times of profound change, revolution, or war, when established political systems are perceived as fragile, unsteady, or on the brink of collapse. These events have reshaped political landscapes, redefined borders, and influenced the course of global history. From the fall of empires to the breakdown of democracies, the world has witnessed moments when the very fabric of political systems seemed poised to tear apart. This essay examines key historical periods when the world, or significant parts of it, feared political collapse, and how these crises have shaped the modern geopolitical order.

A World in Fear of Collapse

Fears of the collapse of the American government are well founded. Exploring the history of world leading governments give us a perspective that can either aid in its recovery or predict its doom.

1. The Roman Empire

The collapse of the Roman Empire remains one of the most significant examples of a political system's disintegration. For centuries, Rome had been the pinnacle of political power, territorial dominance, and military prowess. However, by the 5th century CE, the empire found itself on the brink of collapse, driven by a combination of internal corruption, economic instability, military decline, and external invasions.

The fall of Rome was not a singular event but a slow and painful process that unfolded over centuries. From the third century CE onward, the empire began to experience a series of challenges, including political instability, a series of weak emperors, and power struggles within the imperial elite. The division of the empire into the Western and Eastern Roman Empires in 395 CE, under Emperor Theodosius, left the West vulnerable to external threats.

As the Western Roman Empire faced the continued pressure of invasions by Germanic tribes such as the Visigoths, Vandals, and Ostrogoths, the political system became increasingly fractured. In 476 CE, the last Roman emperor of the West, Romulus Augustulus, was deposed by the Germanic chieftain Odoacer, signaling the formal end of the Western Roman Empire. While the Eastern Roman Empire, later known as the Byzantine Empire, continued for nearly another thousand years, the collapse of the West marked a decisive moment in history.

During this period, there was widespread fear of the collapse of political order across Europe. The fall of Rome created a power vacuum that led to centuries of instability, with the emergence of feudal systems, the rise of the Catholic Church as a political and spiritual authority, and the eventual formation of new kingdoms. In many ways, the fear of political collapse was not limited to Rome; it spread throughout the Mediterranean world, as the empire's influence on trade, culture, and governance unraveled.

2. The French Revolution: Fear of Revolutionary Upheaval

The French Revolution, which began in 1789, is another pivotal moment in history when political collapse seemed imminent, not only for France but for much of Europe. The Revolution was fueled by deep social, economic, and political inequalities. The monarchy, under Louis XVI, faced significant financial crises, exacerbated by France's involvement in the American Revolution and lavish spending at the royal court.

As the Revolution gained momentum, the French monarchy was increasingly viewed as weak and out of touch with the needs of the people. Widespread poverty, food shortages, and growing discontent among the common people sparked uprisings in Paris and other cities. The Estates-General convened in 1789 to address the fiscal crisis, but the commoners, frustrated by their lack of representation, declared themselves the National Assembly, signaling a challenge to royal authority.

The storming of the Bastille on July 14, 1789, marked the symbolic beginning of the Revolution. As the Revolution progressed, France descended into chaos, marked by the execution of King Louis XVI and Queen Marie Antoinette, the Reign of Terror, and the rise of radical political ideologies. The fear of collapse was palpable as the Revolution threatened to engulf not only the monarchy but also the entire political and social order of France. Revolutionary leaders, including Maximilien Robespierre, sought to eliminate perceived enemies of the Revolution through brutal measures, leading to widespread fear, suspicion, and violence.

The Revolution inspired similar uprisings across Europe, and for a time, the future of monarchies and traditional political systems was in question. The fear of revolutionary collapse led monarchs and conservative elites to form coalitions to suppress revolutionary movements, leading to a series of wars known as the Napoleonic Wars.

The French Revolution reshaped Europe politically, establishing the principles of liberty, equality, and fraternity, but it also demonstrated the volatility of political systems during times of upheaval.

3. The Bolshevik Revolution: Fear of Global Communist Revolution

The Bolshevik Revolution of 1917 in Russia marked another critical moment when the world feared political collapse, this time within the context of the Russian Empire and the broader global order. The fall of Tsar Nicholas II and the establishment of the Soviet Union were catalysts for political transformation that would alter the course of history for much of the 20th century.

In the early 20th century, Russia was embroiled in widespread discontent. Economic hardship, military defeats in World War I, and political repression had eroded the legitimacy of the Tsarist regime. The February Revolution of 1917 led to the abdication of Tsar Nicholas II and the establishment of a provisional government. However, the provisional government was unable to address the deep-seated problems facing Russia, and it struggled to maintain control over a restive population.

In October 1917, the Bolsheviks, led by Vladimir Lenin, seized power in a coup that would lay the foundation for the establishment of the Soviet Union. The Bolshevik Revolution was fueled by socialist ideologies, and it called for the overthrow of capitalist systems in favor of a Marxist-Leninist state. The overthrow of the Tsarist regime was a direct challenge to the traditional political order, and the fear of global revolution spread throughout Europe and beyond.

The collapse of the Russian Empire and the rise of Bolshevism prompted fears among other nations that similar revolutions might take hold. Countries with large working-class populations, such as Germany and Hungary, saw uprisings and revolutions of their own, inspired by the Russian example. The fear of communism and the potential collapse of capitalist systems became a central concern for Western powers.

The aftermath of the Bolshevik Revolution led to the Russian Civil War, as various factions, including the White Army (loyal to the Tsar), fought against the Bolshevik Red Army. The eventual victory of the Bolsheviks led to the consolidation of Soviet power, but it also sparked a global ideological divide that would define much of the 20th century, particularly during the Cold War.

4. The Cold War: Fear of Nuclear Collapse

The Cold War, which began after World War II and lasted for several decades, was characterized by a profound fear of political and societal collapse due to the possibility of nuclear war. The United States and the Soviet Union, both superpowers, engaged in an ideological, political, and military struggle that brought the world to the brink of destruction on several occasions.

The fear of nuclear collapse was especially acute during moments such as the Cuban Missile Crisis in 1962, when the world watched as the U.S. and the Soviet Union engaged in a tense standoff over the presence of Soviet nuclear missiles in Cuba. The crisis brought the two superpowers closer than ever to full-scale nuclear war, and the fear of global political collapse was felt across the world.

During this period, both the U.S. and the Soviet Union engaged in massive arms buildups, creating a climate of fear and mutual distrust. The specter of nuclear annihilation was a constant presence, and the threat of political collapse was not just theoretical—it seemed imminent. The development of nuclear weapons, combined with the high-stakes political maneuvering of the Cold War, made the possibility of global collapse a very real concern.

In response, both superpowers engaged in psychological and political campaigns to maintain control over their populations. Propaganda, surveillance, and the suppression of dissent were tools used to keep internal political systems intact. Meanwhile, the fear of communism and the collapse of democracy led to numerous proxy wars in places like Korea, Vietnam, and Afghanistan, as both sides sought to expand their influence.

5. The Fall of the Berlin Wall and the Collapse of the Soviet Union

The final collapse of the Soviet Union in 1991 was another moment when the world watched the disintegration of a major political power. The collapse of the USSR marked the end of the Cold War and the beginning of a new geopolitical order. The fall of the Berlin Wall in 1989, a symbol of the ideological divide between the communist East and the capitalist West, triggered a wave of democratization and independence movements throughout Eastern Europe and beyond.

In the final years of the Soviet Union, the leadership of Mikhail Gorbachev attempted to reform the political system through policies such as perestroika (economic restructuring) and glasnost (political openness). However, these reforms inadvertently hastened the collapse of the Soviet system, as they exposed deep cracks in the political, economic, and social structures of the USSR.

The collapse of the Soviet Union was accompanied by economic turmoil, political instability, and a power vacuum that led to the rise of oligarchs, regional conflicts, and the eventual emergence of the Russian Federation under Vladimir Putin. For many in the West, the collapse of the USSR was seen as the end of the threat of global communism. However, the aftermath of the collapse also generated fears about the instability of the post-Soviet space and the potential for further political fragmentation.

6. The 2008 Financial Crisis: Fear of Economic and Political Collapse

The global financial crisis of 2008 was another instance when the world feared the collapse of political and economic systems. The crisis, triggered by the collapse of major financial institutions, widespread defaults on mortgage loans, and the bursting of the housing bubble, led to economic downturns across the globe. The interconnectedness of global markets and the scale of the crisis prompted fears of a total economic collapse, which in turn raised concerns about the stability of political systems.

In many countries, the 2008 financial crisis led to widespread protests, political instability, and the rise of populist movements. The political fallout from the crisis was felt in the United States, where the election of Barack Obama in 2008 was partly a response to voter anger over the economic collapse. Across Europe, austerity measures were implemented, leading to protests and political unrest, as citizens reacted to the perceived failure of political elites to prevent the crisis.

The fear of political collapse during the financial crisis was not limited to economic factors. It was also a reflection of the growing distrust of political institutions and the sense that the traditional political elite had failed to protect the interests of ordinary citizens.

A History of Political Uncertainty

Throughout history, the world has faced moments of profound fear regarding political collapse. From the fall of ancient empires to the modern-day challenges of economic crises and global conflicts, these moments of uncertainty have shaped the course of history. Political collapse, whether real or perceived, has the potential to trigger widespread societal upheaval, redefine national borders, and alter the trajectory of global events.

As we face new global challenges in the 21st century—whether related to climate change, technological advancements, or rising geopolitical tensions—the fear of political collapse remains a constant undercurrent in global affairs. The lessons of history remind us that political stability is fragile, and the specter of collapse is always present, lurking just beneath the surface of even the most powerful nations and systems.

The fear of societal collapse has been a constant throughout history. During moments of economic, political, or social instability, populations often fear the unraveling of the societal structures that underpin their daily lives. From the fall of great empires to economic depressions, these fears are typically accompanied by widespread anxiety about the future of the nation, civilization, or world at large. Yet, despite these recurring crises, humanity has consistently found ways to assuage these fears and rebuild societal cohesion. By examining historical events and moments of crisis, we can better understand how societies have navigated fears of collapse and emerged more resilient.

1. The Fall of Empires and the Rise of New Powers

One of the most enduring fears of societal collapse has been the fall of empires. Throughout history, the decline of great empires such as the Roman Empire, the Byzantine Empire, and others has generated a fear that civilization itself was collapsing. However, despite the crumbling of these powerful political entities, the collapse often led to new forms of government, social organization, and cultural rejuvenation. The fall of empires and the creation of new political entities were frequently pivotal moments in the historical trajectory of societies.

The Fall of the Roman Empire (476 CE)

The fall of the Roman Empire, especially its western half in 476 CE, is often seen as one of the most significant collapses in world history. The empire had been the center of European political, economic, and military power for centuries, and its disintegration left a vacuum in which disorder and violence seemed inevitable. The Roman Empire's inability to defend its vast borders from barbarian invasions, coupled with internal corruption, political instability, and economic decline, led to its eventual collapse.

However, rather than marking the end of civilization, the fall of Rome gave rise to the medieval period in Europe, which was characterized by feudalism, the spread of Christianity, and the emergence of the Holy Roman Empire. While the political collapse was indeed a traumatic event, the society adapted by creating new political and social structures. The Catholic Church became a central unifying force in Europe, providing stability and guidance during a period of fragmentation. Monasteries preserved knowledge through their libraries, and new kingdoms arose, such as those of the Franks, which would later become the foundation of modern European states.

The Rise of the Byzantine Empire and the Middle Ages

While the fall of Rome in the West was perceived as catastrophic, the Eastern Roman Empire, known as the Byzantine Empire, continued to thrive for nearly a thousand years after the fall of Rome. The Byzantine Empire's survival is often credited to its ability to adapt to changing circumstances. The Byzantines maintained a strong centralized government and a sophisticated bureaucracy, which helped ensure continuity in governance despite external and internal threats.

In the wake of the fall of the Western Roman Empire, the Byzantine Empire acted as a bridge between the ancient classical world and the medieval period, preserving much of Roman law, culture, and intellectual traditions. This preserved knowledge was instrumental in the intellectual and cultural revival that occurred during the Renaissance. Thus, the fear of societal collapse was assuaged not by the return to the old order, but through the gradual development of new political and social structures that ensured continuity and survival.

2. The Resilience of Societies During Economic Crises

Economic crises have historically been another source of widespread fear of societal collapse. These crises—whether they are caused by war, famine, or financial mismanagement—often lead to fears of widespread poverty, political instability, and the dissolution of social order. However, throughout history, societies have demonstrated an extraordinary ability to recover from economic disaster by adapting their systems, restructuring their economies, and finding new ways to promote social cohesion.

The Great Depression and the New Deal

One of the most significant economic crises in modern history was the Great Depression of the 1930s. The stock market crash of 1929 and the subsequent global economic downturn led to widespread unemployment, homelessness, and suffering. Many feared that the depression would lead to the collapse of capitalist economies and the rise of authoritarianism or even communism. In the United States, the fear of political collapse was palpable, as millions of people lost their jobs, banks failed, and social unrest grew.

However, President Franklin D. Roosevelt's New Deal programs sought to address the immediate economic crises through job creation, social welfare programs, and financial reforms. The establishment of Social Security, the expansion of unemployment insurance, and the creation of public works programs helped to stabilize the American economy and restore confidence. Furthermore, the establishment of regulatory bodies like the Securities and Exchange Commission (SEC) and the Federal Deposit Insurance Corporation (FDIC) helped prevent a repeat of the financial excesses that had caused the crash.

By responding to the economic crisis with expansive government intervention and social programs, the United States was able to avoid a collapse of its political and economic systems. The New Deal not only helped to restore confidence in the economy but also contributed to the creation of a stronger social safety net, which mitigated future fears of collapse in the face of economic instability.

3. The Development of Political Systems During Times of War

War has been another source of widespread fear about societal collapse. The devastating impact of wars, especially World War I and World War II, led to fears that entire civilizations could be destroyed. However, societies have often found ways to rebuild and stabilize after such conflicts through the development of new political systems, international cooperation, and social movements.

The Post-World War II Era: The Formation of International Institutions

After the destruction wrought by World War II, much of the world feared that the war's devastation could lead to the collapse of entire nations or even the collapse of civilization itself. The war had decimated Europe, Japan, and parts of Asia, and the death toll was staggering. Many feared that the rise of totalitarian regimes or the onset of another war could lead to the end of democratic governance and international peace.

However, following the war, the global community sought to create a new order to prevent future conflicts and the collapse of democratic societies. The establishment of the United Nations (UN) in 1945 aimed to provide a platform for international diplomacy and peacekeeping. This was coupled with the establishment of new political systems in countries previously under fascist or authoritarian rule. Germany and Japan, for example, adopted democratic constitutions and integrated into the post-war global system, signaling a shift away from the political ideologies that had led to the war in the first place.

The Marshall Plan, which provided financial aid to help rebuild war-torn Europe, played a significant role in stabilizing the economies of European nations and preventing the rise of communist ideologies in the wake of the war. These efforts helped to restore faith in democracy and capitalism, assuaging fears of political collapse in Europe and Japan.

The United States and the Rise of the Welfare State

In the aftermath of the world wars, the United States, along with many European nations, saw the expansion of welfare state policies. These policies were designed to ensure that the state would provide for its citizens' basic needs, such as healthcare, education, and social security. The rise of the welfare state helped to mitigate the fears of political collapse by demonstrating that governments could provide security and stability even in times of economic difficulty or social unrest.

In countries such as the United Kingdom, the creation of the National Health Service (NHS) in 1948 was a pivotal moment in addressing the social and economic needs of the population. Similarly, in the United States, the expansion of social programs, such as Social Security and Medicare, helped to alleviate concerns about the ability of the government to maintain social stability during periods of economic downturn or political upheaval.

4. Social Movements and Grassroots Activism

During periods of political or social upheaval, the fear of societal collapse can often be assuaged through grassroots activism, social movements, and collective action. These movements can offer alternative visions of society and provide a sense of purpose and direction during times of crisis.

The Civil Rights Movement (1950s–1960s)

In the United States, the Civil Rights Movement of the 1950s and 1960s was a response to the widespread systemic racism and discrimination faced by African Americans. The movement emerged during a time of great social upheaval, and many feared that the tensions between races could lead to political instability or even violence. However, through nonviolent resistance, led by figures such as Martin Luther King Jr., and through legal and political reforms, the Civil Rights Movement succeeded in achieving significant progress in securing equal rights for African Americans.

The Civil Rights Act of 1964 and the Voting Rights Act of 1965 were landmark pieces of legislation that helped to address some of the root causes of racial inequality in the United States. By confronting these issues head-on, the movement helped to prevent the collapse of American democratic institutions and provided a model for future social movements around the world.

The Collapse of Apartheid in South Africa

Similarly, the end of apartheid in South Africa in the early 1990s marked a moment when fears of societal collapse were assuaged through collective action, international pressure, and political reform. The apartheid system, which had segregated and oppressed South Africa's black population for decades, had led to widespread unrest and fears of civil war. The international community imposed sanctions on South Africa, and domestic resistance movements, led by figures like Nelson Mandela and Desmond Tutu, advocated for the dismantling of apartheid.

Through negotiations and the eventual release of Mandela from prison, South Africa was able to transition peacefully to a democratic system, avoiding the collapse of its political and social structures. The peaceful end to apartheid was a testament to the power of grassroots activism and the ability of societies to overcome deeply entrenched social and political systems.

Another Trump Presidency

The long-term political implications of the Trump presidency are vast and multifaceted, shaping both the American political landscape and its international relations in ways that will be felt for decades. From the rise of populism to the fracturing of the Republican Party, Trump's presidency introduced a range of changes, some of which were anticipated while others emerged unexpectedly. The presidency of Donald Trump, marked by polarizing rhetoric, contentious policies, and unconventional leadership, has set the stage for profound shifts in American political discourse, governance, and the relationship between the government and the people.

This essay explores the possible long-term political implications of the Trump presidency, focusing on key areas such as political polarization, party realignment, democratic norms, global influence, and the evolution of American identity. By examining these factors, we can better understand how Trump's tenure may reshape the American political system in both the near and distant future.

1. Political Polarization and Its Entrenchment

Trump's presidency amplifies the ideological chasm between the left and the right, contributing to the entrenchment of partisan identities and animosity.

The Role of Media and Social Media

Trump's use of social media, and personal relationships with the controlling members of social media, to communicate directly with the public, bypassing traditional media outlets, has had a lasting effect on how politics is conducted in the U.S. His reliance on social media to shape the narrative and engage with supporters (often in confrontational and incendiary ways) and his support from their billionaire owners significantly altered political communication. His presidency marked the convergence of politics with entertainment, as social media platforms amplified his often controversial messages, further polarizing voters and galvanizing political activism on both sides of the spectrum.

Social media has become an even more potent tool for influencing public opinion, and the Trump presidency is directly linked to the rise of "alternative facts," misinformation, and the creation of echo chambers where individuals are exposed only to viewpoints that align with their preexisting beliefs. This form of communication nurtured political divisions, undermined trust in traditional news sources, and contributed to the spread of false narratives.

The Entrenchment of Political Divides

The Trump presidency not only accelerated the partisan divide but also exacerbated ideological purity within both the Republican and Democratic Parties. Within the GOP, Trump cultivated a political base that embraced populism, nationalism, and anti-establishment rhetoric. This faction became more entrenched, leading to the reshaping of the Republican Party into a more ideologically rigid entity, often placing loyalty to Trump above traditional conservative principles.

On the left, the rise of more progressive candidates, many of whom rejected moderate compromise, was seen as a response to the radicalization of the right. Figures like Bernie Sanders and Alexandria Ocasio-Cortez gained prominence, advocating for policies such as Medicare for All, the Green New Deal, and a progressive overhaul of the American political system. This ideological polarization, seen in the political rhetoric and policy proposals, suggests that the deepening divide between the two major parties may persist for the foreseeable future.

2. The Realignment of the Republican Party

The Trump presidency has had profound and lasting effects on the Republican Party. Prior to Trump's rise, the GOP was dominated by establishment figures who adhered to traditional conservative principles. However, Trump's populist appeal and outsider status disrupted this established order, leading to a redefinition of what it means to be a Republican.

Populism and Nationalism

Trump's appeal to working-class voters, particularly those disillusioned with the political elite, represents a key shift in the GOP's base. His campaign and presidency were marked by a focus on economic nationalism, immigration restriction, and anti-globalist sentiment. Trump's ability to galvanize these voters reshaped the Republican Party's platform and its outreach to minority communities. Many analysts argue that the party has moved away from traditional conservative fiscal policies and toward a more populist, nationalist approach that prioritizes America First policies.

This realignment has been particularly evident in the party's stance on immigration, trade, and foreign policy. Trump's rhetoric on building a border wall and imposing tariffs on foreign nations marked a stark departure from previous GOP platforms that favored free trade and more lenient immigration policies. As the Republican Party became increasingly tied to Trump's populist ideology, traditional conservative voices were often marginalized.

The Role of Trumpism in Future Republican Politics

Even after Trump left office, his influence on the GOP remained palpable. The term "Trumpism" has come to define the new direction of the Republican Party, with many of its leaders and candidates embracing his populist, nationalist agenda. As Trump continued to assert his influence within the party, figures like Florida Governor Ron DeSantis and Texas Senator Ted Cruz built their political careers by adopting similar positions on immigration, economic policy, and cultural issues.

The future of the GOP is likely to remain shaped by Trumpism, with the party divided between Trump loyalists and more traditional conservatives. While some Republican elites seek to reassert control over the party's direction, Trump's populist rhetoric continues to resonate with a significant portion of the electorate, particularly in swing states and rural areas. This could result in a Republican Party that is increasingly hostile to centrism and compromise, instead focusing on winning elections by appealing to the base that supports Trump's vision of American greatness.

3. Erosion of Democratic Norms and the Threat to Institutions

Another critical long-term implication of the Trump presidency is the erosion of democratic norms and the weakening of institutions that undergird the U.S. political system. Trump's disregard for established rules, his challenges to the legitimacy of the electoral process, and his attempts to undermine the rule of law posed significant risks to the democratic fabric of the nation.

The Capitol Riot and the Attack on the Electoral Process

The most dramatic manifestation of the erosion of democratic norms occurred during the January 6, 2021, Capitol riot, which was directly fueled by Trump's false claims of election fraud. By encouraging his supporters to "stop the steal" and reject the results of the 2020 election, Trump cast doubt on the integrity of the democratic process and undermined public faith in the electoral system.

While the events of January 6, 2021, were unprecedented in their violence and audacity, they were also indicative of a broader trend of eroding trust in democratic institutions. Trump's rhetoric during his presidency, particularly around issues such as election security, the media, and the judiciary, fostered a sense of skepticism about the effectiveness of the U.S. government and the impartiality of its institutions. The fallout from the Capitol riot, including the impeachment proceedings and the resulting legal challenges, will likely have lasting consequences for how Americans view their democratic institutions and the importance of respecting electoral outcomes.

Judicial Appointments and Long-Term Impacts on the Judiciary

One of the most lasting legacies of the Trump presidency is his impact on the federal judiciary. Trump appointed three Supreme Court justices, significantly altering the ideological balance of the Court for generations to come. His appointments of Neil Gorsuch, Brett Kavanaugh, and Amy Coney Barrett cemented a conservative majority that will shape the direction of American jurisprudence for decades.

In addition to the Supreme Court, Trump appointed hundreds of federal judges to lower courts, many of whom hold conservative views on issues such as abortion, gun rights, and religious freedoms. These appointments have the potential to influence significant legal battles in the future, with conservative judges shaping rulings on key issues related to voting rights, LGBTQ+ rights, healthcare, and more.

Undermining Trust in Media and Accountability

Trump's repeated attacks on the media, branding them as "fake news" and "the enemy of the people," furthered distrust in institutions of accountability. This rhetoric was designed to delegitimize critical reporting and silence opposition voices. The long-term effect of these attacks has been the erosion of public trust in journalistic outlets, particularly among Trump's base, which increasingly relied on right-wing media outlets for information.

This distrust extends beyond the media to include other critical institutions, such as the Justice Department, the FBI, and intelligence agencies. Trump's attempts to discredit these bodies through personal attacks and conspiratorial claims left lasting scars on the public's perception of their objectivity and credibility. The sustained undermining of these institutions risks creating a fragmented view of reality in the U.S., where different segments of the population have vastly different understandings of facts, further deepening political polarization.

4. Changes in U.S. Foreign Policy and Global Leadership

The Trump presidency marked a shift in U.S. foreign policy, as Trump's "America First" approach prioritized national interests over international alliances and cooperation. Trump's skeptical stance toward multilateralism, his questioning of long-standing alliances such as NATO, and his withdrawal from key international agreements had far-reaching consequences for global stability and America's role on the world stage.

The Decline of Multilateralism

Under Trump, the U.S. pulled out of several international agreements, most notably the Paris Agreement on climate change, the Iran nuclear deal, and the Trans-Pacific Partnership (TPP). These actions signaled a departure from multilateral diplomacy and a return to more isolationist and unilateral policies. While Trump's approach resonated with his populist base, it created fractures in U.S. relations with key allies and undermined global efforts to address issues such as climate change, arms control, and trade.

In the long term, the U.S.'s retreat from multilateralism could pave the way for other global powers, such as China and Russia, to take a more prominent role in shaping international policy. The decline in American leadership could lead to a more fragmented and less cooperative global order, where the U.S. is seen less as a global leader and more as a self-interested power prioritizing its own concerns over collective international action.

The Rise of China and Changing Global Dynamics

Trump's confrontational approach to China, which included imposing tariffs and labeling China a strategic competitor, has had lasting implications for global geopolitics. While his administration aimed to confront China on issues such as trade imbalances, intellectual property theft, and military expansion, it also contributed to the intensification of the U.S.-China rivalry.

The long-term political implications of this rivalry will be felt in the shifting balance of power between the U.S. and China, with both countries vying for dominance in areas such as technology, military influence, and global governance. As China seeks to expand its influence, particularly in regions such as the South China Sea, Africa, and Latin America, the U.S. will face new challenges in maintaining its position as the world's leading superpower.

5. The Legacy of Trump's Populism and Identity Politics

Trump's presidency gave rise to a new wave of populism in the U.S., with an emphasis on nationalism, anti-elitism, and cultural identity. His rhetoric around immigration, race, and American identity became central to his political platform, shaping debates over issues such as multiculturalism, the role of women in politics, and racial justice.

The Persistence of Cultural Divisions

In the long term, Trump's populism has contributed to the persistence of cultural divisions in the U.S. Issues related to race, immigration, and American identity will likely remain contentious, as Trump's rhetoric and policies have mobilized a segment of the population that feels alienated by demographic changes and shifting social values. These divisions could manifest in future electoral battles, as the U.S. continues to grapple with questions of national identity, multiculturalism, and the place of minority groups in American society.

The political implications of the Trump presidency are profound and far-reaching. From deepening polarization and a shifting party landscape to the erosion of democratic norms and changing U.S. foreign policy, Trump's tenure has left an indelible mark on American politics. While it is difficult to predict exactly how these changes will unfold in the coming decades, it is clear that Trump's legacy will shape the direction of the nation for years to come.

The political landscape of the United States has been forever altered.

What Can We Do?

Resilience in the Face of Fear

Throughout history, societies have faced crises that sparked fears of political, social, or economic collapse. However, time and again, humanity has demonstrated resilience and ingenuity in the face of adversity. Whether through the rise of new political systems, the rebuilding of economies, the formation of international institutions, or the power of social movements, these fears have been assuaged through collective action, reform, and adaptation.

The key to overcoming fears of societal collapse has often been the ability of societies to evolve, to adapt to changing circumstances, and to recognize the importance of unity, stability, and cooperation. From the ashes of fallen empires to the aftermath of economic crashes, the story of human history is one of overcoming fear and forging new paths toward progress and resilience.

The Significant Role of Subcultures

Subcultures—often defined as groups that create distinct values, norms, and practices that differ from those of mainstream culture—have historically played a significant role in shaping society. These groups, often born from a sense of marginalization or the desire for alternative ways of living, have contributed to the social, cultural, and political fabric of nations by challenging the status quo, advocating for inclusivity, and fostering creativity. Throughout history, subcultures have acted as agents of change, driving societal progress in ways that may have seemed radical or unconventional at the time but ultimately led to profound positive transformations.

Subcultures are frequently misunderstood or vilified by the mainstream due to their deviation from conventional norms. Yet, many of the social movements that have reshaped societies over time were initially birthed in subcultures. Whether through music, fashion, art, or activism, subcultures can inspire individual expression, challenge oppressive systems, and promote progressive social values. By examining how subcultures have changed society for the better, we can gain a deeper understanding of their lasting impact on human culture and social development.

1. The Role of Subcultures in Challenging Social Norms and Inequalities

One of the most powerful ways in which subcultures can change society for the better is by challenging established social norms, which are often rooted in unequal power structures. Subcultures, especially those that arise in opposition to the mainstream, have been instrumental in critiquing oppressive social hierarchies and advocating for greater equality and justice. These challenges to the status quo often lay the groundwork for broader societal shifts toward inclusivity, civil rights, and individual freedoms.

The Civil Rights Movement and Black Power Subcultures

The Civil Rights Movement of the 1950s and 1960s in the United States is one of the most significant examples of a subculture challenging racial inequalities. While the movement as a whole is often discussed in terms of political activism and public protest, there were also important subcultures within the broader movement that contributed to societal change.

The Black Power subculture, for example, emerged as a reaction to the more moderate Civil Rights Movement spearheaded by leaders such as Martin Luther King Jr. While King advocated for nonviolent civil disobedience, the Black Power movement, led by figures like Malcolm X, Stokely Carmichael, and the Black Panther Party, focused on self-determination, pride, and the empowerment of African Americans. This movement created a subculture that emphasized black cultural identity and pride, rejecting assimilation into white-dominated society. It brought issues such as police brutality, economic inequality, and racial injustice to the forefront of public discourse.

By confronting white supremacy, promoting black pride, and calling for political and economic autonomy, the Black Power movement not only challenged entrenched racial norms but also contributed to lasting changes in American society. The cultural shifts that came from this subculture—such as the embrace of African culture, the popularity of "Afro" hairstyles, and the use of black-centric imagery in media—helped to reshape the national identity, influencing subsequent generations in their pursuit of racial equality.

The LGBTQ+ Movement and the Evolution of Gender Norms

The LGBTQ+ subculture has also played a vital role in challenging heteronormative gender expectations and advocating for the rights of sexual minorities. Historically, LGBTQ+ individuals have been marginalized, stigmatized, and criminalized for their sexual orientations or gender identities. The LGBTQ+ community has long fought for societal acceptance, legal recognition, and equality in marriage, employment, and healthcare. These efforts have reshaped societal attitudes toward sexuality and gender.

The Stonewall Riots of 1969, a pivotal moment in LGBTQ+ history, sparked a larger cultural shift that would lead to the modern LGBTQ+ rights movement. The riots, which took place at the Stonewall Inn in New York City, were a response to police harassment of LGBTQ+ individuals. The subsequent mobilization of LGBTQ+ communities in the aftermath of the riots gave rise to a subculture that would fight for the decriminalization of homosexuality, the right to marry, and social acceptance of diverse sexual orientations and gender identities.

The visibility of LGBTQ+ individuals in popular culture, their increasing representation in the media, and the creation of LGBTQ+ organizations to advocate for policy changes have led to greater social acceptance and legal reforms. Marriage equality, non-discrimination laws, and improved societal understanding of gender fluidity are just a few examples of the transformative effects that this subculture has had on society. As a result, LGBTQ+ people are increasingly seen as equal participants in society, with the right to live freely and authentically.

2. Subcultures and Their Contribution to Artistic and Cultural Innovation

Subcultures are also important drivers of artistic and cultural innovation. Often on the fringes of mainstream society, subcultures create alternative spaces for creativity to flourish. These alternative artistic expressions—whether in music, fashion, visual art, or literature—have the power to influence and transform mainstream culture, challenging conventional aesthetics and inspiring new ways of thinking.

The Punk Rock Subculture

One of the most iconic subcultures that has reshaped modern culture is the punk rock movement. Emerging in the 1970s as a reaction against the excesses of mainstream music and societal complacency, punk rock was characterized by its raw, rebellious energy and anti-establishment attitudes. Punk music, with its fast tempos, stripped-down instrumentation, and provocative lyrics, challenged the polished, commercialized sound of mainstream rock and pop music.

The punk subculture extended beyond music to influence fashion, art, and political activism. Punk's DIY ethos—"Do it yourself"—encouraged individuals to take creative control of their work, whether it was creating their own clothes, producing independent music, or making political statements. Punk fashion, with its leather jackets, torn jeans, and spiked hair, became a symbol of defiance and individualism.

Beyond its aesthetic and political statements, punk rock gave birth to new genres of music and laid the groundwork for subsequent musical movements, including alternative rock, grunge, and indie rock. Punk's embrace of countercultural values and rejection of conformity resonated with young people around the world, leading to a widespread rethinking of what music, art, and culture could be.

Hip-Hop: A Subculture That Transformed Global Culture

Hip-hop, which originated in the South Bronx during the 1970s, is another subculture that has had a profound impact on global culture. Initially born as an artistic movement among marginalized African American and Latino youth, hip-hop quickly grew into a global cultural force. Through its four main elements—rap music, DJing, graffiti art, and breakdancing—hip-hop provided a means for underrepresented groups to express themselves and assert their identity.

Hip-hop's influence on language, fashion, and entertainment is immeasurable. The genre's impact on music has been far-reaching, with rap becoming one of the most commercially successful genres worldwide. Furthermore, hip-hop has reshaped fashion trends, introduced new forms of dance, and given rise to a distinctive visual culture. Graffiti art, which was initially seen as vandalism, is now recognized as a legitimate form of artistic expression, influencing the world of contemporary art.

Hip-hop has also played a pivotal role in giving voice to social and political issues, particularly those related to race, class, and police brutality. Many rap songs address systemic inequality, urban poverty, and the struggles of marginalized communities. By doing so, hip-hop has created a space for social commentary, raising awareness of important issues and sparking conversations about justice and equality.

3. Subcultures and Political Activism: A Path to Social Justice

Subcultures have also played a critical role in fostering political activism, raising awareness of societal injustices, and advocating for transformative change. By organizing around issues of social justice, subcultures have been instrumental in shifting public discourse and influencing policy decisions. These subcultures can inspire individuals to become active participants in the political process, empowering them to fight for their rights and the rights of others.

The Environmental Movement and Earth Liberation Front (ELF)

The environmental movement, which gained significant momentum in the 1960s and 1970s, represents another example of a subculture influencing societal change. The movement was born from a growing concern about pollution, deforestation, and the destruction of natural habitats. In response, activists began to challenge industrial practices and call for greater protection of the environment.

One prominent subculture within the environmental movement is the Earth Liberation Front (ELF), which uses direct action, including acts of civil disobedience, to protest environmental degradation. Although controversial for its use of more radical tactics, ELF and other subcultures within the environmental movement have played an essential role in raising awareness about climate change, advocating for sustainable practices, and challenging corporate practices that harm the environment.

Through grassroots activism and organized campaigns, the environmental movement has brought issues such as climate change, biodiversity loss, and pollution to the forefront of global policy discussions. The movement's influence has led to the adoption of environmental protection laws, the growth of renewable energy industries, and the global recognition of the urgent need to address climate change.

The Feminist Movement and the Fight for Gender Equality

The feminist movement, which emerged as a subculture in the 19th century and gained greater prominence during the 1960s and 1970s, has been another powerful force for societal change. Feminism has long fought for women's rights and gender equality, challenging deeply ingrained patriarchal norms that have historically limited women's opportunities and freedom.

Feminist subcultures have pushed for reproductive rights, gender parity in the workplace, and greater representation of women in politics and media. The #MeToo movement, which gained widespread attention in 2017, is a prime example of a feminist subculture that has created a global conversation about sexual harassment and assault. Through social media and grassroots activism, the #MeToo movement empowered women to share their stories and hold perpetrators accountable, leading to significant shifts in societal attitudes toward sexual violence.

By challenging gender norms and advocating for equality, the feminist movement has helped to reshape social, political, and legal systems, resulting in improved rights and opportunities for women. Feminist subcultures continue to inspire new generations of activists committed to advancing gender justice and dismantling patriarchal structures.

Subcultures as Catalysts for Positive Change

Subcultures, often seen as marginal or deviant, have played an indispensable role in shaping society for the better. Whether through challenging social norms, fostering artistic innovation, or promoting political activism, subcultures have consistently acted as agents of change, pushing society toward greater inclusivity, equality, and justice. By questioning the status quo, advocating for marginalized groups, and creating alternative ways of thinking and living, subcultures have driven progress on a global scale.

While these subcultures may face resistance from mainstream society, their impact cannot be denied. The changes they bring, although sometimes gradual, have the power to transform society in profound and lasting ways. From civil rights and LGBTQ+ acceptance to environmental activism and gender equality, subcultures have not only shaped culture but also made the world a better place for future generations.

The Impact of Local Government

Local governments, often seen as the smaller, less glamorous levels of political administration, play a critical role in maintaining and enhancing the stability of a nation. While national governments receive much of the public's attention, the essential functions carried out at the local level — from managing public services to promoting community engagement and ensuring local security — have a profound influence on the stability of society as a whole. By directly addressing the needs and concerns of citizens, local governments foster a sense of trust and ownership within communities, contributing to social cohesion, economic stability, and effective governance.

Local governments possess the unique ability to connect people to their broader political system. They operate as the first point of contact for citizens with the state and are often responsible for managing the services and programs that most directly affect their daily lives. As a result, local governments can be both a stabilizing and transformative force within the political landscape. This essay will explore the various ways in which local governments positively impact national stability, focusing on areas such as public service provision, economic development, social cohesion, political engagement, and crisis management.

1. Enhancing Public Services and Infrastructure

Local governments are responsible for delivering a wide range of essential services that impact the daily lives of citizens, including education, healthcare, public transportation, housing, waste management, and law enforcement. By efficiently providing these services, local governments contribute to a stable and functioning society, which is crucial for the overall stability of the nation.

Improving Education and Healthcare Access

Education and healthcare are two fundamental services that directly influence the well-being and productivity of a nation's population. Local governments play a key role in ensuring that citizens have access to quality schools, universities, and healthcare facilities. In education, local authorities are often in charge of managing public schools, setting curriculum standards, and supporting teachers. By providing equitable access to education, local governments foster social mobility and reduce inequality, which is essential for maintaining national stability. When local governments invest in education, they are not only improving the future prospects of their communities but also strengthening the human capital of the nation as a whole.

In healthcare, local governments are frequently responsible for running local hospitals, clinics, and public health programs. By ensuring that healthcare is accessible and affordable for all citizens, local governments play a critical role in promoting public health, reducing disease transmission, and preventing social unrest related to health disparities. During times of crisis, such as a pandemic or natural disaster, local governments are often the first responders and the most visible entities in terms of providing assistance. Effective local public health responses can prevent the escalation of health crises, contributing to broader societal stability.

Transportation and Infrastructure Development

Transportation and infrastructure are other critical areas where local governments contribute to national stability. Public transportation systems, road maintenance, waste management, and utilities such as water and electricity are all managed at the local level in many countries. Well-maintained infrastructure ensures that people can move freely, access jobs, and engage in economic activities. In turn, this contributes to the smooth functioning of the economy, reduces poverty, and alleviates social tension that could arise from inadequate resources.

In urban areas, local governments often oversee city planning, zoning, and public housing. By ensuring that communities have access to affordable housing and that cities are well-organized, local governments can help prevent the growth of slums and the exacerbation of social inequality. In rural areas, local governments focus on improving infrastructure like roads and water systems, which ensures that citizens have access to basic services that are essential for maintaining a stable society.

2. Promoting Economic Development

Local governments are also key players in fostering economic stability and development. Economic policies and initiatives implemented at the local level can have far-reaching effects on national economic growth and the reduction of income inequality. Through targeted investment in infrastructure, job creation, small business development, and attracting investment, local governments contribute to sustainable economic growth.

Job Creation and Local Economic Development

Local governments can create jobs by funding and supporting local businesses, promoting entrepreneurship, and establishing favorable business environments. Municipalities can offer incentives for businesses to set up operations, whether through tax breaks, infrastructure support, or workforce training programs. These initiatives promote local employment and increase economic stability, which in turn reduces the likelihood of social unrest caused by high unemployment or economic disparity.

Local governments also play a role in addressing regional economic disparities, ensuring that all areas within a country, whether urban or rural, have access to economic opportunities. By directing investment toward underdeveloped areas, local governments can prevent the polarization of economic power and resources, which often fuels discontent and social instability. This is particularly important in developing nations, where large portions of the population may live in poverty due to a lack of local economic opportunities.

Supporting Small and Medium Enterprises (SMEs)

Small and medium enterprises (SMEs) form the backbone of many economies, particularly in emerging markets. Local governments support SMEs by creating policies that reduce bureaucratic red tape, providing microfinancing, offering technical assistance, and fostering a conducive business environment. These policies can stimulate innovation, foster competition, and help diversify local economies, leading to the creation of wealth and prosperity at the grassroots level.

When local governments facilitate the success of SMEs, they are helping to stabilize national economies by ensuring that economic opportunities are distributed widely across society, reducing the reliance on a few large corporations or industries. Furthermore, a thriving small business sector contributes to the resilience of local economies, making them more adaptable to changing economic conditions and global trends.

3. Strengthening Social Cohesion and Political Stability

Local governments play an indispensable role in fostering social cohesion, which is vital for the stability of a nation. Social cohesion refers to the ability of individuals within a society to live together harmoniously, despite differences in culture, ethnicity, and socioeconomic status. By providing a platform for community engagement and promoting inclusive policies, local governments help create more integrated, peaceful communities.

Inclusive Community Engagement

Local governments are closer to the people they serve, which allows them to understand the specific needs and concerns of different communities. Through town halls, community outreach programs, and local councils, local governments facilitate direct communication between citizens and the government. This engagement helps to build trust and confidence in government institutions, reducing the risk of alienation and social unrest.

By addressing the needs of marginalized and vulnerable populations—whether they be ethnic minorities, low-income families, or people with disabilities—local governments can prevent the emergence of social divides that might threaten national stability. Inclusive policies that promote equal access to services and opportunities contribute to a more cohesive society where people feel valued and represented.

Conflict Resolution and Community Safety

Local governments are on the front lines of maintaining peace and order within their communities. In cases of civil unrest, local governments are often the first to respond with security measures, negotiations, and mediation efforts. By maintaining law and order at the local level, these governments prevent minor tensions from escalating into broader conflicts that might destabilize entire regions or nations.

Local law enforcement agencies, often under the direction of local governments, are tasked with protecting citizens from crime and ensuring that justice is served fairly. When local police forces are well-trained, accountable, and operate with integrity, they foster a sense of security that reinforces national stability. Additionally, local governments can play an active role in conflict resolution, bringing together various community leaders to mediate disputes and prevent violence.

Promoting Cultural Diversity and Tolerance

In increasingly multicultural societies, local governments play a key role in promoting cultural diversity and tolerance. They can foster community integration by supporting programs that celebrate the contributions of different ethnic and cultural groups. Local governments can also facilitate dialogue between communities, addressing issues of discrimination or xenophobia before they escalate into more significant societal problems.

By providing opportunities for cultural exchange, supporting immigrant populations, and advocating for inclusive policies, local governments contribute to a more peaceful and tolerant society. This cultural integration helps create a sense of national unity, which is essential for the overall stability of the nation.

4. Crisis Management and National Stability

Local governments are often the first responders to emergencies, whether they be natural disasters, public health crises, or economic shocks. Their ability to manage crises effectively can mitigate the impact on national stability, preventing local issues from spiraling into larger-scale disasters.

Disaster Preparedness and Response

Local governments are responsible for disaster preparedness, response, and recovery efforts. They develop emergency plans, coordinate relief efforts, and ensure that resources are distributed to affected populations. In the event of a natural disaster such as an earthquake, flood, or hurricane, local governments often take the lead in organizing rescue operations and providing immediate assistance to victims. Their prompt and effective action helps to minimize the loss of life and prevent widespread panic, contributing to national stability.

The ability of local governments to manage and recover from crises builds resilience within communities, ensuring that they are better prepared for future challenges. In the face of recurring environmental disasters, for example, local governments can implement long-term strategies for disaster mitigation, such as strengthening infrastructure, promoting sustainable land use practices, and investing in climate adaptation initiatives.

Public Health Crisis Management

Local governments are also critical in managing public health crises, such as epidemics or pandemics. During the COVID-19 pandemic, local governments were responsible for implementing lockdowns, distributing vaccines, and ensuring the smooth functioning of essential services. By taking proactive steps to contain the spread of disease, local governments help protect public health and reduce the risk of widespread societal disruption.

In addition to responding to immediate crises, local governments often invest in preventive healthcare measures, such as immunization programs, health education, and disease surveillance. These measures reduce the likelihood of future outbreaks, contributing to the long-term health and stability of the nation.

The positive impact of local government on the stability of a nation cannot be overstated. Local governments play a pivotal role in enhancing public service provision, fostering economic development, promoting social cohesion, and managing crises. By addressing the specific needs of communities and facilitating inclusive, responsive governance, local governments create a foundation for national stability and prosperity.

While national governments often garner the most attention, it is at the local level where many of the most significant and lasting changes occur. The ability of local governments to engage with citizens, provide essential services, and respond to crises ensures that societies remain resilient in the face of challenges. Ultimately, the positive contributions of local government help to create more stable, cohesive, and prosperous nations.

The Effect of Individual Citizens

The stability of a nation is often attributed to political institutions, economic systems, and social structures. However, one of the most profound contributors to the long-term stability of a nation is the active and engaged participation of its citizens. When individuals take ownership of their rights and responsibilities, contribute to their communities, advocate for social change, and hold governments accountable, they form the bedrock of a resilient society. This essay explores the numerous ways in which individual citizens can positively affect the stability of their nations, examining their roles in political participation, social cohesion, economic prosperity, community building, and crisis response.

1. Political Participation and Governance

A stable nation is rooted in the active participation of its citizens in the political process. While elected representatives and government officials hold formal power, the engagement of the populace in governance is what ensures the legitimacy and responsiveness of political systems. From voting and running for office to peaceful protest and community organizing, individual citizens play an indispensable role in shaping the political landscape of their country.

Voting and Elections

The act of voting is one of the most direct ways in which individual citizens contribute to the stability of a nation. In democratic systems, elections serve as a mechanism by which the population expresses its preferences and ensures that political power is distributed in accordance with the will of the people. The active participation of citizens in elections helps maintain political stability by ensuring that the government remains accountable to its constituents and reflects the diverse interests of society.

When citizens vote, they engage in a peaceful process of decision-making that strengthens the democratic system and helps prevent political instability. A lack of voter engagement, on the other hand, can lead to disenfranchisement, erode trust in the political system, and increase the risk of authoritarianism. Thus, voter participation is not just a civic duty but a vital tool for maintaining the health and stability of the nation.

Holding Governments Accountable

Beyond voting, individual citizens have a crucial role to play in holding governments accountable for their actions. This can be achieved through public discourse, advocacy, and protest. When citizens raise their voices against government policies that they perceive as unjust, inefficient, or corrupt, they ensure that those in power remain responsive to the needs of the population.

Citizens who engage in peaceful protests or civic movements help to highlight societal issues that may otherwise be overlooked or ignored by those in power. Whether advocating for civil rights, environmental protection, or economic equality, the actions of individual citizens ensure that the government does not become complacent or authoritarian. When governments are held accountable by their citizens, they are more likely to adopt policies that reflect the collective interests of the people, contributing to social harmony and national stability.

Community Organizing and Civic Engagement

Individuals who engage in grassroots organizing and community activism play an important role in strengthening the fabric of civil society. Whether through local civic organizations, volunteer work, or non-governmental organizations (NGOs), these citizens build bridges between people from diverse backgrounds, create networks of mutual support, and contribute to the social capital of the nation. By actively participating in the governance process, individuals ensure that their voices are heard and that the needs of their communities are addressed.

In this way, citizens help create a more vibrant and dynamic democratic process. Community organizing fosters a sense of collective responsibility, encourages collaboration, and strengthens democratic values. These efforts, in turn, contribute to political stability by promoting inclusivity, reducing polarization, and fostering a spirit of cooperation.

2. Social Cohesion and National Unity

Another essential role that individual citizens play in ensuring the stability of a nation is through the promotion of social cohesion and national unity. In diverse societies, where multiple ethnic, religious, and cultural groups coexist, it is the responsibility of citizens to foster understanding, tolerance, and mutual respect. When citizens take active steps to create a harmonious society, they reduce the potential for social conflict and division, which can destabilize a nation.

Promoting Tolerance and Respect for Diversity

In pluralistic societies, individual citizens contribute to national stability by advocating for tolerance and respecting diversity. People who actively seek to understand and appreciate cultural differences are more likely to contribute to a harmonious society where conflicts are resolved peacefully. Citizens who engage in interfaith dialogues, celebrate multiculturalism, and challenge prejudices play a crucial role in promoting national unity.

When citizens resist divisive rhetoric and embrace inclusivity, they help prevent the rise of extremism, xenophobia, or ethnic tension. National stability depends on citizens' ability to transcend group identities and work together for the common good. In this way, individuals act as stabilizing forces, fostering an environment where everyone, regardless of background, feels valued and included.

Volunteering and Philanthropy

Volunteering and philanthropy are two ways in which citizens contribute to the social cohesion and well-being of their country. By volunteering their time and resources to charitable causes, individuals help to address the social needs of marginalized groups, contribute to disaster relief efforts, and strengthen social bonds. In times of crisis, volunteers provide critical support to emergency services and community organizations, helping to alleviate suffering and reduce social unrest.

Through philanthropy, individuals can contribute to the alleviation of poverty, the improvement of education, and the development of healthcare systems. These acts of kindness and generosity have a ripple effect, creating stronger, more resilient communities. When citizens come together to support each other, they foster a culture of mutual care, which enhances social stability.

Building Strong Social Networks

Citizens who participate in community events, neighborhood groups, and local activities help build social networks that are essential for societal stability. These networks provide emotional and practical support in times of need, create spaces for collective problem-solving, and foster a sense of belonging. By engaging with one another and working collaboratively, individuals form a social fabric that is more resilient to challenges.

Strong social networks are particularly important during times of crisis, such as natural disasters, economic downturns, or political instability. When individuals trust one another and feel connected to their communities, they are more likely to act in ways that support the collective good. These social connections contribute to national stability by enhancing cooperation, reducing isolation, and encouraging mutual support.

3. Economic Contributions and Prosperity

The stability of a nation is also closely linked to the economic well-being of its citizens. When individuals actively participate in the economy, contribute to the workforce, and engage in entrepreneurship, they help create a thriving economy that underpins national stability. Economic prosperity fosters social stability by reducing poverty, lowering unemployment, and increasing opportunities for upward mobility.

Workforce Participation and Job Creation

One of the primary ways in which individual citizens contribute to economic stability is by participating in the workforce. Citizens who contribute to the economy by working in various industries, from healthcare to manufacturing to technology, help drive productivity and growth. As the workforce grows and diversifies, a nation is better equipped to respond to economic challenges and maintain stability in the face of changing global conditions.

Moreover, citizens who start businesses or engage in entrepreneurship stimulate economic activity and create jobs for others. Entrepreneurs help to diversify the economy, foster innovation, and increase competition, which leads to a more dynamic and resilient economy. By contributing to job creation, citizens reduce unemployment and the potential for social unrest caused by economic hardship.

Paying Taxes and Supporting Public Services

Taxes are the primary source of revenue for most governments, and individual citizens play a critical role in ensuring that governments have the financial resources needed to provide essential public services. By paying taxes, citizens contribute to the funding of education, healthcare, infrastructure, law enforcement, and social welfare programs. These services are fundamental to maintaining the stability of society, as they ensure that citizens have access to the resources they need to lead healthy, productive lives.

When citizens fulfill their tax obligations, they help strengthen the nation's economic foundation, reduce debt, and improve public services. In doing so, they promote long-term stability by supporting the functioning of the state and ensuring that government policies are sustainable.

Encouraging Sustainable Practices

In recent years, individual citizens have played an increasingly important role in promoting sustainable economic practices. Through responsible consumption, investing in green technologies, and advocating for environmental protection, individuals help to ensure that economic growth does not come at the expense of future generations. Sustainable practices contribute to national stability by ensuring that resources are managed responsibly and that environmental degradation does not destabilize ecosystems, economies, and societies.

Individuals can also influence government policies by advocating for environmental regulations, supporting renewable energy initiatives, and pushing for greater investment in sustainable industries. These efforts help create an economy that is not only prosperous but also resilient to future challenges such as climate change.

4. Crisis Response and National Resilience

In times of national crisis—whether from natural disasters, public health emergencies, or political instability—individual citizens are often the first to respond, mobilizing quickly to support their communities and mitigate the impact of the crisis. Citizens' resilience, adaptability, and willingness to collaborate in times of adversity are vital for maintaining national stability.

Responding to Natural Disasters

Natural disasters, such as hurricanes, earthquakes, and wildfires, can have devastating effects on a nation's infrastructure and social fabric. However, the quick and coordinated response of individual citizens can help mitigate the impact of these disasters. Citizens often volunteer in disaster relief efforts, help evacuate vulnerable populations, and assist with rebuilding efforts in the aftermath of a catastrophe.

In addition to direct aid, citizens can help raise awareness about the risks of natural disasters and advocate for improved disaster preparedness and response systems. By contributing their time, expertise, and resources, individual citizens ensure that their communities remain resilient in the face of environmental challenges.

Public Health Emergencies

During public health crises, such as the COVID-19 pandemic, individual citizens play a vital role in mitigating the spread of disease and protecting public health. Citizens who follow public health guidelines, such as wearing masks, practicing social distancing, and getting vaccinated, contribute to the collective effort to contain the outbreak and prevent widespread illness. These actions help reduce the burden on healthcare systems and ensure that the nation's health infrastructure remains functional and effective.

In addition, citizens can volunteer to help distribute vaccines, assist in contact tracing efforts, and provide care for vulnerable populations. By taking individual responsibility for public health, citizens ensure that their nation can weather health crises and emerge stronger and more united.

Disobedience

Civil disobedience, the act of intentionally breaking laws or regulations to protest perceived injustice, plays a nuanced role in stabilizing society. While often viewed as a disruptive force, civil disobedience can catalyze necessary societal change and contribute to long-term stability by addressing systemic issues that, if left unresolved, might lead to greater unrest or inequality.

At its core, civil disobedience operates on the principle of nonviolent resistance. The acts of protest are typically intended to raise awareness about unjust laws or policies without resorting to violence, thus distinguishing it from outright rebellion or anarchy. By calling attention to unfair practices or discrimination, civil disobedience can prompt public discourse and, in some cases, lead to the reevaluation of laws and practices that no longer serve the greater good.

In the case of Luigi Mangione, who shot and killed United Health CEO Brian Thompson, the act caused UnitedHealthcare to revise its practices almost immediately. Mangione felt the shooting was justified and necessary to effect change in a business model whose purpose has evolved to limit life-saving health care for its own clients.

When society is burdened by unjust laws, civil disobedience can act as a pressure valve that prevents larger-scale social upheaval. For example, movements like the American Civil Rights Movement in the 1960s utilized civil disobedience to challenge segregation and racial injustice. The protests, such as the sit-ins and marches, demonstrated the moral and ethical shortcomings of discriminatory laws, eventually leading to legislative change such as the Civil Rights Act of 1964 and the Voting Rights Act of 1965. In this way, civil disobedience contributed to a more just society, and the legal and social changes that followed reinforced societal stability by fostering greater equality and integration.

Moreover, civil disobedience can serve as a reflection of the health of a democracy. A vibrant democracy allows room for dissent and protest, where citizens can voice dissatisfaction without resorting to violence. If governments acknowledge these acts as legitimate forms of civic expression, they reinforce the principles of free speech and public participation. When marginalized voices are heard and their grievances addressed, societal cohesion and trust in institutions are strengthened.

However, civil disobedience alone does not guarantee stability. It requires a responsive government that is open to reform and a society willing to engage in constructive dialogue. The ultimate role of civil disobedience in stabilizing society lies in its ability to foster awareness, spark necessary reforms, and challenge outdated or unjust systems—making it an essential tool in ensuring a fair and balanced society that evolves to meet the needs of all its members.

Positive Collective Action

The positive impact of individual citizens on the stability of a nation cannot be overstated. From political participation and social cohesion to economic contributions and crisis response, citizens play a crucial role in maintaining the stability and resilience of their countries. When individuals engage in the political process, advocate for social change, build strong communities, contribute to economic prosperity, and respond to crises, they create a stable foundation on which nations can thrive.

In a world that is increasingly interconnected and complex, the actions of individual citizens are more important than ever in promoting national stability. By taking responsibility for their own well-being and contributing to the common good, citizens ensure that their nations remain stable, prosperous, and resilient in the face of challenges. Ultimately, the collective actions of individuals form the bedrock of national stability, fostering a society that is cohesive, responsive, and adaptable.

How Social Media Could Positively Affect the Stability of America

Social media has become an integral part of daily life in America, influencing everything from how people communicate and consume information to how political campaigns are run and social movements gain traction. While social media has often been criticized for spreading misinformation, exacerbating political polarization, and fostering divisiveness, it also holds significant potential to positively impact the stability of the United States. By harnessing the power of social media in constructive ways, it can strengthen democratic processes, promote social cohesion, enhance civic engagement, and facilitate collective action in addressing national challenges.

This essay explores the various ways in which social media can contribute to the stability of America. Specifically, it examines how social media can enhance political engagement, increase transparency and accountability in government, foster a sense of community, address social issues, promote education, and provide platforms for positive activism. By analyzing both current and potential future uses of social media, this essay argues that, when used responsibly, social media has the capacity to strengthen the fabric of American democracy and society.

1. Enhancing Political Engagement and Civic Participation

One of the most direct ways in which social media can contribute to the stability of America is by enhancing political engagement and encouraging civic participation. Social media platforms such as Twitter, Facebook, Instagram, and TikTok provide people with the tools to engage with the political process, stay informed about current events, and share their views with a wide audience. By enabling direct communication between citizens and political leaders, social media can increase transparency, make government actions more accessible, and foster a more informed electorate.

Encouraging Voter Participation

Social media has proven to be an effective tool for encouraging voter participation. During elections, political campaigns and advocacy groups use social media platforms to mobilize voters, share information about voting processes, and promote specific candidates or causes. Social media allows campaigns to reach a broad and diverse audience, particularly younger generations who may not otherwise be engaged with traditional forms of political communication. By creating targeted content, organizing online events, and engaging with voters directly through social media, campaigns can increase voter turnout and ensure that more Americans participate in the democratic process.

Social media platforms can also play a critical role in combating voter suppression by providing citizens with accurate information about their rights and how to vote. For example, social media campaigns that educate voters about voter ID laws, absentee voting, and polling locations can help reduce confusion and barriers to voting. As a result, social media has the potential to make the voting process more inclusive, ensuring that all eligible citizens can exercise their right to vote.

Facilitating Public Discourse and Debate

In addition to promoting voter participation, social media can also serve as a forum for public discourse and debate. By enabling citizens to express their opinions, share ideas, and engage in discussions about important political and social issues, social media fosters an open and inclusive dialogue. This platform for dialogue helps to strengthen democratic values by encouraging diverse viewpoints, enhancing political awareness, and stimulating critical thinking.

Through social media, individuals can engage directly with political leaders, participate in online town halls, or take part in public petitions and campaigns. These interactive features promote a sense of ownership over political decisions and give citizens a voice in shaping public policy. Social media also allows people to organize events, such as protests or rallies, and to raise awareness about issues they care about, increasing public participation in the democratic process.

While online debates can sometimes become heated and polarizing, social media also provides the opportunity to foster constructive conversations by bringing together people from different backgrounds and perspectives. Social media platforms can encourage empathy and understanding by facilitating exchanges that challenge pre-existing beliefs and assumptions, thereby promoting a more informed and engaged electorate.

2. Increasing Transparency and Accountability in Government

Social media plays an increasingly important role in increasing transparency and accountability in government. The ability to instantly share information with the public allows for greater scrutiny of political actions and public policies. This level of transparency can help ensure that government officials remain accountable to the people they serve and that corruption or misconduct is more likely to be exposed.

Direct Communication with Citizens

Social media allows government officials, lawmakers, and political leaders to communicate directly with their constituents, bypassing traditional media channels. This direct line of communication enables politicians to share updates on legislation, policy changes, and public initiatives in real time. It also allows citizens to ask questions, express concerns, and provide feedback directly to their elected representatives.

For example, many politicians and government agencies use platforms like Twitter and Facebook to keep their constituents informed about upcoming votes, changes in law, or the status of critical public services. These platforms offer a space for citizens to interact with their elected officials and hold them accountable for their actions, creating a more transparent and responsive government.

Exposing Corruption and Mismanagement

Social media also has the power to expose corruption, government mismanagement, and human rights violations. Through platforms like Twitter, YouTube, and Instagram, whistleblowers and citizen journalists can share firsthand accounts, videos, and other forms of evidence that might otherwise go unnoticed by traditional media outlets. This democratization of information can make it more difficult for government officials to hide unethical practices or misconduct.

For example, viral social media posts have been instrumental in exposing instances of police brutality, government cover-ups, and corporate malfeasance. In many cases, social media has led to public outcry, investigations, and even legal action. By allowing citizens to share their observations and report on events as they unfold, social media can serve as an important tool for ensuring that governments and institutions remain accountable to the public.

Mobilizing for Change

In addition to exposing wrongdoing, social media provides a platform for citizens to organize around issues of corruption and government accountability. Citizens can use social media to share petitions, raise awareness about public policy failures, and organize collective actions to demand change. These grassroots efforts can lead to meaningful political and social reforms, as demonstrated by movements like #MeToo, Black Lives Matter, and climate justice campaigns.

Social media allows ordinary citizens to have a significant impact on the political agenda by rallying support, mobilizing protest movements, and influencing public opinion. These collective efforts can put pressure on governments to address social injustices, increase transparency, and enact policies that benefit the public good. In this way, social media serves as a powerful tool for holding elected officials accountable and driving positive change.

3. Fostering a Sense of Community and Social Cohesion

In a large, diverse nation like the United States, social media has the potential to foster a sense of community and social cohesion. Social media platforms connect individuals from various backgrounds, cultures, and geographical locations, enabling them to share experiences, ideas, and support. In times of crisis or national disaster, social media can also serve as a tool for solidarity and collective action, helping communities come together in ways that strengthen national unity.

Creating Support Networks

Social media enables people to form and join online communities based on shared interests, experiences, or values. These virtual communities provide a space for people to seek advice, share information, and offer support to one another. For example, social media has played a key role in supporting mental health initiatives by providing people with access to online resources, support groups, and peer counseling. These networks help individuals feel less isolated and more connected to others who are experiencing similar challenges.

Additionally, social media allows people to rally around common causes, whether it's a charitable initiative, environmental activism, or humanitarian relief efforts. By coming together in online spaces, individuals can collaborate on projects, fundraise for important causes, and create positive social change. This sense of collective action and shared purpose can help reinforce social cohesion and strengthen national solidarity.

Promoting Inclusivity and Diversity

Social media also plays a role in promoting inclusivity and celebrating diversity. Through online platforms, individuals from marginalized or underrepresented groups can share their stories, raise awareness about discrimination, and amplify their voices. By providing a platform for diverse perspectives, social media helps foster a more inclusive society where people from different racial, ethnic, religious, and socio-economic backgrounds feel seen and heard.

Social media campaigns focused on social justice, LGBTQ+ rights, gender equality, and racial equity have helped bring about significant cultural and political shifts. These movements highlight the importance of respecting human rights and promoting fairness, which can contribute to greater social stability. By amplifying diverse voices and advocating for inclusivity, social media strengthens the sense of belonging and unity that is essential for a stable society.

Providing a Platform for Constructive Dialogue

While social media is often criticized for fostering echo chambers and polarization, it also has the potential to facilitate constructive dialogue and bridge divides. Social media platforms offer opportunities for individuals with differing views to engage in discussions, challenge each other's ideas, and find common ground. Online debates, when conducted respectfully and thoughtfully, can foster a deeper understanding of different perspectives, reduce polarization, and promote civil discourse.

For example, many organizations use social media to create spaces for dialogue on important societal issues, such as immigration reform, healthcare access, and criminal justice. These conversations can be a stepping stone toward greater understanding, empathy, and cooperation. When citizens engage in thoughtful discussions online, they help to create a more informed and compassionate society, which ultimately contributes to national stability.

4. Facilitating Collective Action for Social Good

Social media has proven to be an effective tool for organizing and promoting collective action on a wide range of social issues. By connecting people across geographic and ideological boundaries, social media allows individuals to work together toward common goals. This collective action can have a powerful impact on public policy, social norms, and national priorities, ultimately contributing to the stability of the nation.

Supporting Social Movements and Activism

Social media has played a key role in advancing social movements that seek to address inequality and injustice. Campaigns like #BlackLivesMatter, #MeToo, and #ClimateStrikes have demonstrated the power of social media in mobilizing millions of people around the world to advocate for change. These movements have raised awareness about critical issues such as police brutality, sexual harassment, and climate change, and have led to tangible changes in policy and societal attitudes.

By providing a platform for activists to organize, share information, and raise awareness, social media empowers individuals to take action and make their voices heard. Whether through online petitions, virtual protests, or social media campaigns, collective action on social media can have a direct impact on national debates and public policy.

Facilitating Disaster Response and Relief

In times of crisis, social media has the potential to mobilize people for disaster response and relief efforts. Whether it's a natural disaster, humanitarian crisis, or public health emergency, social media can be used to coordinate volunteers, share critical information, and fundraise for those affected. For example, during hurricanes, wildfires, and other natural disasters, social media platforms have been instrumental in organizing emergency response efforts, coordinating donations, and connecting survivors with resources.

The ability to rapidly mobilize people in times of need ensures that communities can respond effectively to crises, thereby enhancing national resilience. Social media can help create a sense of unity and shared purpose as individuals come together to support one another during difficult times.

Potential

While social media has its challenges, its potential to positively affect the stability of America is undeniable. By enhancing political engagement, increasing transparency, fostering social cohesion, and facilitating collective action, social media can strengthen American democracy and society. When used responsibly and with purpose, social media can contribute to a more informed electorate, a more inclusive society, and a more responsive government. In times of crisis, it can serve as a tool for solidarity and collective action, helping communities unite and respond to national challenges.

Ultimately, social media's impact on the stability of America depends on how it is used. By prioritizing civil discourse, combating misinformation, and fostering inclusivity, social media can play a vital role in maintaining a strong, cohesive, and stable nation.

Face-to-Face Communication

In an increasingly digital and interconnected world, face-to-face communication may seem like an outdated mode of interaction. Yet, in the context of the United States, where political divisions, social unrest, and community fragmentation are growing concerns, face-to-face communication holds the potential to foster understanding, cooperation, and long-term societal stability. Face-to-face interactions enable individuals to engage on a deeper, more personal level, build stronger relationships, and foster a sense of community and solidarity that is often lost in digital exchanges.

This essay explores how face-to-face communication can positively impact the stability of America by examining its role in enhancing political discourse, strengthening social cohesion, improving mental health, reducing polarization, promoting civic engagement, and facilitating problem-solving. By understanding the profound impact that face-to-face communication can have on American society, it becomes clear that fostering meaningful in-person interactions is essential to the well-being of the nation.

1. Strengthening Political Discourse and Deliberation

The political landscape in the United States is often marked by deep divisions, contentious debates, and increasing polarization. While social media platforms and news outlets have become dominant venues for political engagement, they can also exacerbate these divisions by creating echo chambers where individuals are exposed only to viewpoints that align with their own. Face-to-face communication offers a more direct, personal, and empathetic space for engaging in political discourse, which can lead to more thoughtful deliberation and a better understanding of differing perspectives.

Encouraging Civil Dialogue

In contrast to online platforms, where anonymity and lack of non-verbal cues can fuel hostile and polarized interactions, face-to-face communication encourages civil dialogue. When people engage in person, they are more likely to consider the emotions, body language, and tone of their conversation partner, leading to more respectful and thoughtful exchanges. Studies have shown that face-to-face conversations tend to be more empathetic and constructive, as individuals are less likely to resort to insults, dehumanization, or misinformation when interacting in person.

By encouraging civil discourse in face-to-face settings, individuals are better equipped to discuss complex and sensitive political issues, such as healthcare, immigration, and economic policy, in a way that respects the perspectives of others. This kind of dialogue can lead to a more informed and empathetic electorate, reducing political tensions and fostering a more collaborative political culture. For example, town hall meetings, local debates, and community forums provide an opportunity for citizens to engage in meaningful, direct communication with policymakers and fellow citizens, allowing for productive discussions and solutions.

Promoting Cross-Party Collaboration

Face-to-face communication is also essential for bridging political divides and fostering cross-party collaboration. In today's polarized political environment, individuals often only interact with those who share their political views. As a result, misunderstandings, mistrust, and resentment between political parties have grown. Face-to-face interactions, however, offer an opportunity for individuals to find common ground, discuss shared values, and collaborate on issues of mutual concern.

Research has demonstrated that people are more likely to cooperate and compromise in person than in digital spaces. When individuals from different political backgrounds meet face-to-face, they are more likely to form personal connections, empathize with one another, and engage in more productive problem-solving. This can lead to more bipartisan policies and solutions that promote national unity and stability.

2. Building Social Cohesion and Trust

Social cohesion is crucial for maintaining stability in any society. In the United States, social fragmentation, mistrust in institutions, and a breakdown of community ties have contributed to rising social unrest. Face-to-face communication plays a key role in rebuilding social bonds, fostering trust, and creating a sense of belonging. By facilitating direct, personal interactions, face-to-face communication helps individuals form deeper relationships and develop a shared sense of responsibility for the well-being of their communities and the nation as a whole.

Fostering Empathy and Understanding

One of the primary benefits of face-to-face communication is its ability to foster empathy. In-person interactions allow individuals to see and experience the emotions of others, which can lead to a deeper understanding of different perspectives and life experiences. Empathy is essential for building strong, cohesive communities, as it enables individuals to appreciate the challenges faced by others and work together to address shared concerns.

In the context of the United States, where political, racial, and economic divides often create barriers to cooperation, face-to-face communication can help break down these walls. When people engage with one another in person, they are less likely to reduce others to stereotypes or oversimplified narratives. Instead, they recognize the complexity of individuals' lives and experiences. This shared empathy can lead to stronger relationships, a greater sense of community, and a reduction in social tensions.

Building Trust in Institutions

Trust in government and societal institutions has been steadily declining in the United States, contributing to political instability and dissatisfaction with public officials. Face-to-face communication can play a crucial role in rebuilding trust by fostering transparency, openness, and accountability. When citizens have the opportunity to meet with their elected representatives in person, they are more likely to feel heard, respected, and understood.

Local governments, community organizations, and civic groups can use face-to-face meetings to engage directly with citizens, listen to their concerns, and work together to find solutions to local problems. This level of engagement builds trust and shows that government is responsive to the needs of the people. Town halls, community discussions, and neighborhood meetings can promote a sense of shared responsibility and mutual respect, making citizens more likely to trust government institutions and participate in the political process.

3. Enhancing Mental Health and Well-being

The mental health of a nation's citizens is a crucial factor in its overall stability. In recent years, the United States has seen an increase in mental health challenges, including depression, anxiety, and social isolation. These issues are often exacerbated by digital communication, which can contribute to feelings of loneliness, disconnection, and stress. Face-to-face communication offers an antidote to these challenges by providing opportunities for meaningful social interactions that promote emotional well-being and resilience.

Combating Social Isolation

Social isolation is one of the leading contributors to mental health issues in the United States. As more individuals engage in online communication and spend less time in face-to-face interactions, they risk losing the social connections that are essential for emotional health. Face-to-face communication, however, helps combat isolation by providing opportunities for individuals to engage with their peers, form supportive networks, and strengthen their sense of belonging.

In-person interactions are particularly important for older adults, who are often more vulnerable to loneliness and isolation. Social programs that encourage face-to-face engagement, such as senior centers, community groups, and volunteer organizations, help reduce feelings of loneliness and provide individuals with opportunities to connect with others in meaningful ways. These social connections can improve mental health, increase feelings of happiness, and reduce the risk of depression.

Reducing the Negative Effects of Technology

While technology has brought many benefits, it has also introduced challenges to mental health, particularly among younger generations. Social media, in particular, can contribute to anxiety, self-esteem issues, and the pressure to present a curated, idealized version of oneself. Face-to-face communication, in contrast, offers a more authentic and supportive environment for social interaction. When people communicate in person, they can express themselves more freely, without the constant comparisons or filters that often characterize online communication.

Research has shown that face-to-face interactions promote the release of oxytocin, a hormone that fosters trust, bonding, and emotional well-being. These interactions can lead to stronger relationships and a more supportive social network, which in turn improves mental health and resilience. By prioritizing face-to-face communication, communities can reduce the negative effects of technology and foster environments where individuals feel valued, supported, and understood.

4. Promoting Civic Engagement and Community Building

Civic engagement is essential for maintaining a healthy democracy and ensuring that citizens have a say in the decisions that affect their lives. While digital platforms have made it easier for people to engage in political activism, face-to-face communication remains a vital tool for building community involvement, encouraging volunteerism, and promoting active citizenship. By engaging in person, individuals can form stronger connections with their neighbors, collaborate on local initiatives, and work together to solve common problems.

Encouraging Volunteerism and Civic Participation

Face-to-face communication is particularly effective in encouraging volunteerism and community involvement. When individuals interact in person, they are more likely to be inspired to contribute to the well-being of their community. Community organizations, local charities, and civic groups often rely on in-person interactions to recruit volunteers, coordinate events, and foster a sense of shared responsibility. These activities help build a culture of civic participation, where individuals are motivated to take action and support the common good.

For example, local clean-up efforts, food drives, and neighborhood watch programs provide opportunities for citizens to engage with one another in person and contribute to the betterment of their communities. These volunteer activities create a sense of ownership and pride in one's community, which strengthens social bonds and promotes stability.

Fostering Stronger Communities

In-person communication plays a crucial role in building stronger, more resilient communities. By interacting face-to-face, individuals are able to develop a sense of trust, camaraderie, and mutual support that is difficult to replicate through online interactions. Strong communities are essential for addressing local challenges, such as poverty, crime, and access to healthcare, as they provide a network of individuals who can work together to find solutions.

Community centers, local clubs, and social organizations provide spaces for people to gather, share ideas, and collaborate on projects. These in-person interactions foster a sense of belonging and encourage individuals to take an active role in the well-being of their community. The stability of a nation depends on the strength of its communities, and face-to-face communication is a key element in building that strength.

5. Facilitating Problem-Solving and Conflict Resolution

One of the most significant ways that face-to-face communication can positively impact the stability of America is by facilitating problem-solving and conflict resolution. In a country as large and diverse as the United States, conflicts are inevitable. Whether they are political disagreements, social tensions, or interpersonal disputes, finding ways to resolve conflicts peacefully and productively is essential for maintaining national stability.

Promoting Negotiation and Compromise

Face-to-face communication is essential for negotiation and compromise, two critical elements of conflict resolution. In person, individuals are better able to communicate their needs, listen to others, and reach agreements that satisfy all parties. In political settings, face-to-face negotiations can lead to bipartisan agreements and the development of policies that reflect the diverse interests of the American public.

In the context of social and interpersonal conflicts, face-to-face communication allows individuals to express their emotions, clarify misunderstandings, and work together to find mutually agreeable solutions. These interactions promote empathy, reduce hostility, and foster a sense of shared responsibility for resolving conflicts in a way that benefits everyone.

Creating Safe Spaces for Dialogue

Face-to-face communication also creates a safe space for dialogue, where individuals can engage in difficult conversations about sensitive issues such as race, inequality, and immigration. When these conversations take place in person, they are more likely to lead to understanding and healing, as individuals can address their concerns directly and work together to find common ground. These dialogues can help break down barriers, reduce tensions, and promote social harmony.

Relationship Building

Face-to-face communication plays a pivotal role in fostering stability in America by encouraging civil discourse, promoting social cohesion, improving mental health, increasing civic engagement, and facilitating conflict resolution. While digital communication has its place in modern society, the value of in-person interactions cannot be overstated. By prioritizing face-to-face communication, individuals can strengthen their relationships, build trust in institutions, and contribute to a more collaborative, inclusive, and stable society.

In a time when political polarization, social unrest, and mental health challenges are prevalent, face-to-face communication offers a powerful antidote to these problems. Through meaningful, direct interactions, citizens can bridge divides, resolve conflicts, and work together to create a stronger, more resilient America. By investing in face-to-face communication, America can build a future of unity, empathy, and stability for generations to come.

America's Allies

The United States, a global superpower, has long played a significant role in shaping world events, promoting democracy, and providing leadership on the international stage. However, even the most powerful nations are not immune to crises, whether they are political, economic, or social in nature. In times of crisis, the stability of a nation can be threatened, not just by internal strife but also by global geopolitical dynamics. During such turbulent moments, the role of America's allies becomes crucial. Allies are nations with whom the U.S. shares strategic interests, values, and common goals. They can offer vital support in stabilizing America during periods of crisis by providing economic, diplomatic, military, and moral assistance.

America's allies can help stabilize the country in times of crisis. By drawing on historical examples, current geopolitics, and potential future scenarios, we will discuss the critical roles allies can play in stabilizing the U.S. when it faces internal and external challenges. From fostering diplomatic solutions to providing economic support and military assistance, the role of international partnerships has never been more important.

1. Diplomatic Support and International Cooperation

Diplomacy is one of the primary ways in which America's allies can help stabilize the country in times of crisis. The U.S. has long depended on its allies for diplomatic support in global negotiations, conflict resolution, and maintaining the international order. In times of domestic or international turmoil, strong diplomatic alliances can help the U.S. find solutions to pressing issues, both internal and external.

Mediation and Conflict Resolution

In periods of political polarization or social unrest, diplomatic channels can offer avenues for constructive dialogue. America's allies can help mediate internal conflicts by offering neutral ground for discussions or proposing frameworks for peaceful resolution. For example, European allies such as the United Kingdom, France, and Germany could provide valuable diplomatic insight, having dealt with similar issues of political division and social upheaval within their own countries. These nations' experience in managing internal conflict, maintaining unity, and upholding democratic values can provide valuable lessons and frameworks for the U.S. to consider in navigating crises.

Furthermore, allies can help stabilize the U.S. by promoting international cooperation and facilitating peaceful dialogue between opposing factions within the U.S. Global forums such as the United Nations, NATO, and the G7 can provide platforms for America to engage with other nations in ways that promote dialogue and understanding, especially when domestic political tensions threaten to escalate. Diplomatic support from global allies can help diffuse tensions both within the U.S. and in its interactions with the rest of the world.

Strengthening Global Institutions and Alliances

In times of crisis, whether caused by economic instability, a natural disaster, or a global health crisis such as a pandemic, international cooperation becomes essential. America's allies can help stabilize the U.S. by ensuring the continued strength of global institutions and alliances that uphold democratic norms, peace, and security. For example, NATO has long served as a collective defense alliance, which not only protects its members but also ensures stability by acting as a deterrent against external threats. Similarly, organizations such as the

World Trade Organization (WTO) and the United Nations (UN) offer platforms where global governance structures can address issues that impact the U.S. and its allies.

When global crises threaten national stability, a coordinated international response that includes diplomatic efforts from allies can provide the U.S. with the backing it needs to maintain global order and stability. Through multilateral cooperation, America's allies can help craft solutions that mitigate the effects of crises, whether through the enforcement of sanctions, diplomatic pressure, or the resolution of conflicts through international law and norms.

2. Economic Assistance and Recovery

America's economic stability is closely linked to global trade and investment. During times of economic crisis, the U.S. may find itself facing significant challenges such as recession, rising unemployment, or financial instability. In these situations, America's allies can play a critical role in providing economic support and facilitating recovery efforts.

Financial Aid and Support

One of the most direct ways in which allies can help stabilize the U.S. during an economic crisis is through financial assistance. Historically, financial assistance from allied nations has been instrumental in helping countries recover from financial turmoil. For example, during the aftermath of the 2008 global financial crisis, European countries, Japan, and other allies worked with the U.S. to implement recovery programs that included monetary stimulus, economic reforms, and global trade agreements to stabilize the world economy. This global cooperation allowed for the stabilization of financial markets and the prevention of a deeper economic downturn.

In times of future economic crises, such as a severe recession or depression, America's allies can extend financial aid or help facilitate loans through international financial institutions like the International Monetary Fund (IMF) and the World Bank. They can also work with the U.S. to implement cooperative economic policies that stimulate growth, such as coordinating fiscal stimulus packages, opening up trade opportunities, and ensuring the free flow of investment.

Trade and Investment Partnerships

Economic crises often lead to the imposition of protectionist measures, which can harm global trade and exacerbate financial instability. In such times, allies can help stabilize the U.S. by maintaining open trade channels, investing in U.S. industries, and ensuring that global supply chains remain intact. Nations such as Canada, Mexico, Japan, and members of the European Union are critical trading partners for the U.S., and their continued engagement in trade relations can mitigate the effects of economic downturns.

Moreover, by strengthening trade relationships with allied nations, the U.S. can ensure that the flow of goods, services, and capital continues unabated, even during periods of crisis. This can provide a buffer against domestic economic downturns and foster a more resilient economy that can recover more quickly.

Stimulating Innovation and Technology

America's allies can also play a role in helping the U.S. maintain its leadership in technological innovation. In times of economic or societal crisis, the U.S. may face challenges in remaining competitive on the global stage. By collaborating with allies on research and development, technology sharing, and innovation initiatives, America can ensure that it continues to lead in sectors such as artificial intelligence, clean energy, biotechnology, and cybersecurity.

Allies such as Germany, Japan, and the United Kingdom have made significant strides in technology, and through partnerships and joint ventures, they can help the U.S. access cutting-edge research and infrastructure. In times of crisis, this collaboration can provide a much-needed economic boost and a path forward for recovery, strengthening America's global standing and ensuring that it remains competitive in an increasingly complex global economy.

3. Military Assistance and National Security

The role of military alliances, particularly through NATO and other bilateral defense agreements, is another critical aspect of how America's allies can help stabilize the U.S. during times of crisis. While the U.S. military is one of the most powerful in the world, it can benefit from international military cooperation, especially in situations where the threat to national security is multifaceted or global in nature.

Collective Defense and Security

In times of external threats, whether from military aggression, terrorism, or cyber-attacks, America's allies can provide critical military support to help ensure the nation's security. NATO's Article 5, which stipulates that an attack on one member is an attack on all, is a foundational element of the alliance's collective defense strategy. Should the U.S. face external aggression or increased security threats during a crisis, NATO allies can provide military assistance, intelligence sharing, and support in maintaining security at home and abroad.

Furthermore, the U.S. can benefit from its allies' expertise in unconventional warfare, counter-terrorism operations, and cyber defense. For example, European allies such as the U.K. and France have extensive experience in counter-terrorism efforts, which could prove vital in helping the U.S. navigate crises related to domestic terrorism or foreign attacks.

Humanitarian Assistance and Disaster Response

America's allies can also provide humanitarian assistance in times of national crisis. In the event of a natural disaster, terrorist attack, or public health emergency such as a pandemic, foreign allies can assist the U.S. by providing medical supplies, disaster relief teams, and logistical support. For example, during Hurricane Katrina, countries like Canada and the U.K. sent aid, including medical teams, supplies, and funds, to help in the recovery efforts.

Similarly, in the event of a global health crisis, allies can share crucial medical resources and knowledge. The ongoing COVID-19 pandemic highlighted the importance of global cooperation in public health, as many countries provided medical supplies, vaccines, and expertise to help the U.S. address the public health emergency. In times of national disaster or crisis, such international collaboration ensures that the U.S. has the resources and support necessary to respond effectively.

4. Moral and Ideological Support

Finally, America's allies can play an important role in stabilizing the U.S. by offering moral and ideological support. In times of political or social turmoil, when the U.S. is facing challenges to its democratic institutions, alliances with nations that share similar values of freedom, democracy, and human rights can provide solidarity and help reaffirm the nation's commitment to these principles.

Supporting Democratic Institutions and Values

When the U.S. faces internal challenges to its democratic institutions, such as electoral crises, political corruption, or threats to freedom of speech, allies can help reinforce the importance of upholding democratic values. For instance, European countries, which have rich traditions of democracy and rule of law, can provide diplomatic pressure and public support for democratic practices, helping the U.S. address domestic challenges while preserving its foundational values.

Moreover, in times of political polarization, America's allies can serve as examples of political systems that have successfully navigated similar crises. By sharing strategies for managing social and political divisions, maintaining the rule of law, and engaging in democratic dialogue, allies can offer insights and guidance that help the U.S. navigate its own challenges.

Building a Global Coalition for Peace and Stability

Finally, when America faces global criticism or isolation, its allies can help build a global coalition for peace and stability. In times of international crisis, such as conflicts, economic collapses, or human rights violations, America's allies can work together to ensure that the U.S. is not left standing alone. This collective approach ensures that the U.S. is part of a global community working toward common goals of peace, security, and prosperity.

World Outlook

In times of crisis, the stability of a nation is not solely reliant on its internal mechanisms. America's allies play a critical role in offering support, whether through diplomatic assistance, economic cooperation, military alliances, or moral backing. From helping mediate political disputes and fostering dialogue to providing economic recovery programs and military support, America's allies have proven time and again that they are key players in the stability of the nation.

In an increasingly interconnected world, the U.S. cannot afford to navigate crises in isolation. By leveraging the strength of its alliances and maintaining strong relationships with countries that share its values, the United States can better navigate the challenges it faces, ensuring that it remains a beacon of stability, democracy, and leadership on the global stage. The importance of America's allies in times of crisis cannot be overstated, and their contributions are essential to maintaining the country's long-term stability and resilience.

Organizations Working for Positive Change in America

Throughout the history of the United States, numerous organizations have been integral in driving positive change, improving societal conditions, and fostering justice. These organizations span a wide array of issues, from civil rights and social justice to environmental conservation and economic empowerment. In the face of ongoing challenges, including political polarization, racial inequality, economic disparity, climate change, and public health crises, a growing network of non-profits, advocacy groups, grassroots organizations, and community-driven initiatives are working to promote meaningful change and create a more inclusive, sustainable, and equitable society.

This essay explores the vital work of these organizations, highlighting their contributions to American society, examining their approaches, and considering how their efforts can serve as a model for future progress. These organizations encompass a variety of focus areas, including racial justice, economic equity, environmental sustainability, healthcare access, education, and political reform.

1. Civil Rights and Social Justice Organizations

The struggle for civil rights and social justice has been a hallmark of American history, with various organizations pushing for the protection of the rights of marginalized communities, particularly Black Americans. Civil rights movements have paved the way for landmark legal victories and cultural shifts in the United States. Today, several organizations are continuing this important work, tackling systemic racism, promoting equality, and advocating for the disenfranchised.

The American Civil Liberties Union (ACLU)

Founded in 1920, the ACLU is one of the oldest and most prominent civil rights organizations in the United States. Its mission is to defend and preserve the individual rights and liberties guaranteed to all Americans by the Constitution. The ACLU works on a broad range of issues, including free speech, voting rights, racial justice, reproductive rights, LGBTQ+ rights, and immigrants' rights. The organization has been instrumental in challenging unconstitutional laws, defending civil liberties in court, and advocating for policies that ensure greater fairness and equality.

One notable example of the ACLU's work was its involvement in the landmark case *Brown v. Board of Education*, which led to the desegregation of public schools. Today, the ACLU is involved in fighting voter suppression, advocating for criminal justice reform, and defending the rights of marginalized communities in the face of rising political and social tensions.

Black Lives Matter (BLM)

Black Lives Matter is both a movement and an organization that emerged in 2013 after the acquittal of George Zimmerman, the man who killed Trayvon Martin, a Black teenager. Founded by Patrisse Cullors, Alicia Garza, and Opal Tometi, BLM is a global network of activists working to address systemic racism and violence against Black people. The movement gained significant momentum following high-profile incidents of police violence against Black individuals, such as the killings of Michael Brown, Eric Garner, and George Floyd.

BLM advocates for a society where Black lives are valued and protected, and it works to dismantle systems of oppression, including those within the criminal justice system. Through protests, advocacy, and policy reform efforts, Black Lives Matter has been a driving force behind the national conversation on racial inequality, police brutality, and justice reform.

The NAACP (National Association for the Advancement of Colored People)

Founded in 1909, the NAACP is one of the oldest civil rights organizations in the United States. The NAACP has been instrumental in challenging discriminatory laws and practices through litigation, advocacy, and public education. It played a key role in the legal battle that resulted in the *Brown v. Board of Education* decision, which declared that racial segregation in public schools was unconstitutional.

Today, the NAACP works on issues such as voting rights, criminal justice reform, healthcare equity, and education reform. The organization's activism is centered around its mission to achieve political, educational, social, and economic equality for all people, particularly for African Americans.

2. Economic Empowerment and Equity Organizations

Economic disparity remains one of the most pervasive challenges facing the United States, with wealth inequality at levels not seen since the Great Depression. Many organizations are working to reduce economic inequities, promote fair wages, and provide access to resources that can uplift disadvantaged communities.

The Economic Policy Institute (EPI)

The Economic Policy Institute, established in 1986, is a think tank dedicated to promoting policies that raise the economic status of low- and middle-income Americans. The EPI conducts research and advocates for policies that address economic inequality, wage stagnation, and the erosion of labor rights. Through its work, the organization aims to ensure that the U.S. economy works for all Americans, not just the wealthy elite.

The EPI focuses on issues such as income inequality, job quality, labor standards, and education. Their research on the impact of tax policy, corporate behavior, and globalization on working families is essential for understanding how economic policies affect everyday Americans and for pushing forward legislative changes that benefit the broader population.

The United Way

Founded in 1887, the United Way is one of the largest nonprofits in the world, focusing on creating positive community change by improving education, promoting financial stability, and improving health. The United Way works with local partners across the country to tackle issues such as childhood education, housing instability, healthcare access, and food insecurity.

Through its extensive network of volunteers and donors, the United Way has been successful in directing resources to the communities that need them most. The organization helps individuals and families achieve financial independence through job training, housing support, and access to education. By promoting collaboration between government agencies, businesses, and community organizations, the United Way plays a key role in fostering long-term community development.

The Center for Economic and Policy Research (CEPR)

The Center for Economic and Policy Research is an economic research organization that works to promote policies that reduce inequality and enhance opportunities for all Americans. CEPR focuses on issues such as wage growth, healthcare access, labor rights, and fiscal policy.

By providing policymakers with data-driven insights and advocating for pro-labor, pro-worker policies, CEPR helps to build an economy that works for everyone, particularly those on the lower rungs of the economic ladder.

One of the key areas CEPR has focused on is the disparity in wages between workers and corporate CEOs, with research showing that the growing gap between the top earners and the rest of the workforce has significant implications for social mobility and economic fairness. CEPR's work advocates for a more equitable distribution of wealth, greater protection for workers, and policy changes that improve the economic conditions of disadvantaged groups.

3. Environmental Sustainability and Climate Change Organizations

The fight against climate change and the push for environmental sustainability have become central issues for a range of organizations working to ensure a livable planet for future generations. The increasing frequency of natural disasters, the loss of biodiversity, and the rise in extreme weather events have made the work of environmental organizations more urgent than ever.

The Sierra Club

Founded in 1892, the Sierra Club is one of the oldest and most influential environmental organizations in the United States. The Sierra Club has worked for over a century to protect public lands, reduce pollution, and advocate for policies that promote clean energy and environmental sustainability. The organization was instrumental in the creation of national parks, including the establishment of the Grand Canyon as a national park.

Today, the Sierra Club continues its advocacy work, focusing on fighting climate change, protecting natural habitats, and transitioning to renewable energy sources. Through grassroots organizing, legal challenges, and lobbying, the Sierra Club works to influence policy decisions at the local, state, and federal levels to protect the environment and ensure the health and safety of all Americans.

350.org

350.org is a global grassroots movement dedicated to addressing the climate crisis by reducing carbon dioxide concentrations in the atmosphere to 350 parts per million (ppm). Founded by environmentalist Bill McKibben in 2008, 350.org mobilizes people worldwide to demand action on climate change, particularly from governments and corporations. The organization has organized mass protests, climate strikes, and lobbying efforts aimed at pushing for stronger environmental policies.

350.org has also worked to shift the conversation around climate change, emphasizing the importance of a just transition to a clean energy economy that prioritizes equity and fairness for marginalized communities. By focusing on grassroots movements and building coalitions, 350.org is driving a global movement that seeks to address both the environmental and social impacts of climate change.

The Natural Resources Defense Council (NRDC)

The Natural Resources Defense Council is a nonprofit environmental organization that works to protect the planet's wildlife, natural resources, and ecosystems. NRDC's mission is to safeguard the Earth's resources by advocating for stronger environmental protection laws, promoting sustainable practices, and addressing the threats posed by climate change and pollution.

The NRDC works on issues such as air and water quality, wildlife conservation, clean energy, and climate change. Its work includes litigation, policy advocacy, and public education to advance environmentally responsible solutions that benefit both people and nature.

4. Healthcare Access and Public Health Organizations

Access to healthcare remains one of the most pressing issues in America, with millions of Americans lacking adequate insurance and facing financial barriers to necessary medical care. Several organizations are fighting for affordable healthcare, improving public health, and addressing health disparities in underserved communities.

The Kaiser Family Foundation (KFF)

The Kaiser Family Foundation is a nonprofit organization that conducts in-depth research on healthcare issues in the United States, including healthcare reform, insurance coverage, and health disparities. KFF works to provide policymakers, the public, and health professionals with accurate data and analysis to inform decisions about healthcare policy.

Through its research, KFF has helped shape the national conversation around healthcare access, particularly with regard to the Affordable Care Act (ACA). By focusing on policy analysis, KFF provides valuable insights into how changes in healthcare policy can affect different populations, particularly those who are vulnerable or underserved.

Planned Parenthood

Planned Parenthood is one of the largest reproductive health organizations in the United States, providing a range of services to men, women, and families, including birth control, STI screenings, cancer screenings, and abortion services. Founded in 1916, Planned

Parenthood has long advocated for reproductive rights and gender equality, focusing on empowering individuals to make informed choices about their sexual and reproductive health.

The organization's advocacy efforts have been pivotal in shaping policies related to reproductive healthcare, including the fight for access to birth control, safe and legal abortion, and comprehensive sex education. Planned Parenthood continues to be a major player in the ongoing fight to protect reproductive rights, particularly in the face of increasing attacks on abortion access.

5. Education and Youth Empowerment Organizations

Education is a cornerstone of American democracy, and numerous organizations are working to ensure equitable access to quality education for all students, particularly those from low-income and minority communities.

Teach for America

Teach for America (TFA) is a nonprofit organization that recruits recent college graduates and professionals to teach in underserved schools across the country. Its mission is to close the educational achievement gap by placing passionate and talented educators in communities that need them most. TFA focuses on creating a pipeline of educators who are committed to educational equity and providing students with the skills they need to succeed.

Since its founding in 1990, Teach for America has placed thousands of teachers in schools serving low-income communities. Through its alumni network and ongoing efforts, TFA is working to reform the educational system and ensure that all students have access to high-quality education, regardless of their socioeconomic background.

The Bill & Melinda Gates Foundation

The Bill & Melinda Gates Foundation is one of the world's largest philanthropic organizations, and education is one of its primary focus areas. The foundation works to improve global education systems, with a focus on increasing access to higher education, improving K-12 education, and ensuring that students from underserved backgrounds can succeed academically.

The Gates Foundation has made significant investments in improving education outcomes, including supporting innovations in teaching, investing in teacher development, and advocating for education policy reforms at the local, state, and national levels.

The work of organizations striving for positive change in America is diverse, far-reaching, and essential to the well-being of society. From addressing civil rights issues to advocating for economic equity, environmental sustainability, and accessible healthcare, these organizations are vital to the stability of current society.

Organizations That Can Reassure Nervous Americans in an Uncertain Political Environment

In times of political instability, national crises, or significant social change, it is natural for individuals and communities to feel nervous, anxious, or uncertain about the future. In the United States, as political polarization deepens and public trust in government institutions fluctuates, there is a growing need for organizations that provide reassurance, stability, and support to American citizens. These organizations help create a sense of continuity, safeguard democratic principles, and address critical issues that impact individuals' daily lives, ensuring that Americans can feel a sense of agency and confidence in an unpredictable political landscape.

From grassroots advocacy groups to national think tanks and international NGOs, a variety of organizations are working diligently to foster hope, promote civic engagement, and provide essential services that reinforce a strong, functioning democracy. This essay explores organizations that are playing vital roles in reassuring Americans by addressing concerns related to political instability, economic anxiety, social justice, healthcare, and national unity. Through their efforts, these organizations not only mitigate fear but also offer a foundation for moving forward in times of uncertainty.

1. Promoting Civic Engagement and Strengthening Democracy

One of the most effective ways to reassure nervous Americans is by fostering a sense of participation and involvement in the democratic process. When people feel they have a voice in shaping their government, they are less likely to feel alienated or fearful about political outcomes. Several organizations work to promote civic engagement, voter participation, and political literacy, helping citizens navigate the political landscape with confidence and clarity.

The League of Women Voters

Founded in 1920, the League of Women Voters (LWV) is a nonpartisan organization that works to empower voters and defend democratic principles. While originally focused on securing the vote for women, today the LWV works on a wide array of issues related to voting rights, election integrity, redistricting reform, and promoting civic engagement across all demographics. The organization provides resources for voter registration, information on candidates and issues, and supports reforms to improve the electoral process.

By advocating for policies that ensure free, fair, and transparent elections, the League of Women Voters reassures Americans that the democratic process is functioning properly. In an era when trust in elections has been challenged, the LWV's efforts to provide nonpartisan, unbiased information to voters help restore confidence in the system and ensure that all citizens are well-informed and able to exercise their rights.

FairVote

FairVote is a nonprofit organization that advocates for electoral reforms aimed at improving the fairness and effectiveness of U.S. elections. It is particularly focused on issues like ranked-choice voting, electoral representation, and reducing gerrymandering. By working to improve the structure of the electoral system, FairVote helps ensure that all Americans, regardless of political affiliation, can have confidence that their votes count and that their interests are being fairly represented in government.

Ranked-choice voting, which FairVote promotes, allows voters to rank candidates by preference rather than choosing a single candidate. This system has the potential to lead to more representative election outcomes, reduce negative campaigning, and encourage a broader range of candidates to run for office. By advocating for such reforms, FairVote offers a path toward a more inclusive and transparent electoral process.

2. Supporting Social Justice and Equality

Social justice organizations play a critical role in reassuring Americans who are concerned about inequality, discrimination, and the erosion of civil rights. These organizations work to protect marginalized communities, fight for racial and gender equality, and address structural injustices that threaten the social fabric of the nation. Their advocacy and direct action ensure that America's democracy works for everyone, not just the privileged few.

The American Civil Liberties Union (ACLU)

Founded in 1920, the ACLU has been at the forefront of defending civil liberties and constitutional rights in the United States. Its work spans a wide range of issues, including free speech, voting rights, racial justice, LGBTQ+ rights, reproductive rights, and criminal justice reform. The ACLU's mission to defend the rights of individuals against overreach by the government provides an essential check on state power, reassuring Americans that their fundamental freedoms are being protected, no matter how turbulent the political climate.

In times of political uncertainty, the ACLU serves as a powerful reminder of the constitutional principles upon which the nation was built. By challenging unjust laws, defending protestors, and standing up for the rights of vulnerable communities, the ACLU reassures citizens that the protection of civil rights remains a core American value.

The NAACP (National Association for the Advancement of Colored People)

The NAACP, founded in 1909, is the nation's oldest and largest civil rights organization, focused on addressing the systemic challenges faced by African Americans and other communities of color. Through legal advocacy, grassroots organizing, and political mobilization, the NAACP works to ensure that all people have equal access to justice, education, and economic opportunity.

In times of political instability or social unrest, the NAACP serves as an anchor for those seeking justice and equality. Its long-standing commitment to fighting for policies that promote racial equity and its ongoing work to challenge discriminatory practices in policing, voting, and employment provide reassurance to communities who fear their rights may be under threat.

The Southern Poverty Law Center (SPLC)

The SPLC is a nonprofit organization dedicated to tracking and exposing hate groups, advocating for civil rights, and promoting tolerance. Through its extensive legal work and research on hate crimes, the SPLC is a crucial player in fighting against extremism and ensuring that America remains a place where people of all backgrounds can live without fear of violence or discrimination.

The SPLC's work is especially important in times of rising political polarization or when hate-based ideologies gain traction in public discourse. By highlighting the dangers of hate groups and advocating for stronger protections against discrimination, the SPLC reassures Americans that their government is actively working to safeguard the rights and safety of vulnerable communities.

3. Addressing Economic Anxiety and Promoting Stability

Economic instability is one of the most significant sources of anxiety for Americans, especially during periods of political uncertainty. Organizations that focus on economic justice, workers' rights, and poverty alleviation play an essential role in reassuring Americans who fear for their financial futures.

The Economic Policy Institute (EPI)

The Economic Policy Institute, founded in 1986, is a think tank focused on researching and advocating for policies that improve the economic conditions of working Americans. EPI provides critical data and analysis on issues such as wage stagnation, income inequality, labor rights, healthcare, and the economic effects of trade and immigration policy. Its work helps Americans understand the broader economic forces shaping their lives and provides evidence-based solutions to address economic disparities.

By highlighting the importance of fair wages, affordable healthcare, and accessible education, EPI reassures citizens that there are practical policy solutions available to improve their economic prospects. Its research also underscores the need for greater investment in the middle and lower classes, ensuring that Americans can feel confident in policies that promote shared prosperity.

United Way

United Way is one of the largest nonprofit organizations in the world, working to improve the health, education, and financial stability of communities across the U.S. By partnering with local organizations and businesses, United Way helps ensure that individuals and families have access to resources such as job training, financial literacy programs, emergency assistance, and affordable housing.

For Americans facing financial uncertainty or who are struggling with the economic effects of political instability, United Way offers a safety net. Its community-based work ensures that the most vulnerable populations are supported, helping to reduce economic anxiety and reassure individuals that they are not alone in times of crisis.

The Center for American Progress (CAP)

The Center for American Progress is a progressive think tank that focuses on policies to create a fairer and more just economy. CAP works on issues such as income inequality, affordable housing, healthcare, and job creation. By providing detailed research and policy proposals, CAP helps policymakers craft solutions to improve the economic well-being of all Americans, especially those struggling to make ends meet.

In times of political turmoil, CAP provides a vision for a more equitable future. By advocating for policies that increase economic opportunity for disadvantaged groups and strengthen the middle class, CAP reassures Americans that their government is working toward a more inclusive and sustainable economy.

4. Fostering National Unity and Rebuilding Trust

The political divisions that have deepened in recent years pose a significant threat to national unity. Organizations focused on bridging these divides and fostering social cohesion are essential for reassuring Americans who are worried about the future of their country.

The Bridge Alliance

The Bridge Alliance is a network of more than 80 organizations working to promote cross-partisan dialogue, strengthen democratic institutions, and foster cooperation among Americans from different political backgrounds. The Alliance believes that the future of American democracy depends on citizens being able to engage in respectful conversations across party lines, listen to one another, and work together to solve common challenges.

In times of political crisis, the Bridge Alliance helps Americans rebuild trust in one another and in their democratic institutions. Through its programs, events, and initiatives, the Bridge Alliance fosters a sense of common purpose, reminding citizens that they share fundamental values despite their political differences.

The National Institute for Civil Discourse (NICD)

The NICD is a nonpartisan organization dedicated to improving civil discourse and reducing political polarization. Through research, public education campaigns, and events that promote respectful dialogue, NICD works to restore a sense of unity and shared purpose in a politically divided country. The organization's efforts are particularly important in times of political uncertainty, where public discourse can become heated and divisive.

By providing platforms for constructive dialogue and promoting the values of tolerance, respect, and compromise, the NICD reassures Americans that political disagreement does not have to lead to animosity or division. Instead, it emphasizes that the nation's strength lies in its ability to have difficult conversations and come together to address challenges.

In an uncertain political environment, Americans need organizations that can offer reassurance, guidance, and support. From promoting civic engagement and protecting civil rights to addressing economic anxiety and fostering national unity, these organizations play a critical role in maintaining stability and helping individuals navigate political turbulence. By providing a sense of agency, fostering trust in democratic institutions, and advocating for policies that promote justice and equality, these organizations help ensure that Americans remain resilient in the face of uncertainty.

Through their collective efforts, they offer hope, reaffirm democratic values, and remind citizens that, even in the most challenging times, positive change is possible. Whether through direct action, policy advocacy, or community support, these organizations continue to play a vital role in shaping the future of the United States, reassuring citizens that their voices matter, their rights are protected, and their country can remain a beacon of hope and democracy for all.

Fear of Societal Collapse

The fear of societal collapse is a deeply rooted concern that, for many, evokes feelings of helplessness, anxiety, and despair. Whether stemming from political instability, economic uncertainty, environmental crises, or technological disruptions, the fear of a world descending into chaos can weigh heavily on an individual's mental health and worldview. In times of social, political, or environmental turbulence, these fears can become overwhelming, especially for individuals who feel powerless in the face of such massive challenges. However, there are numerous techniques and strategies that can help calm someone experiencing these fears, guiding them toward a more grounded, rational perspective.

This essay will explore various techniques to soothe the fear of societal collapse, offering psychological, practical, and philosophical approaches that can help individuals regain a sense of control and inner peace. These techniques focus on fostering resilience, cultivating mindfulness, encouraging community involvement, and offering hope through action.

1. Understand the Root Causes of the Fear

Before attempting to calm someone who is afraid of societal collapse, it is crucial to understand the root causes of their fear. This fear may stem from a variety of sources, including:

- **Political Instability**: Uncertainty surrounding political decisions, leadership, or international conflicts can make individuals feel as though society is on the brink of breakdown.

- **Economic Uncertainty**: Rising inequality, inflation, unemployment, or the fear of an economic crash can contribute to the perception of impending societal collapse.

- **Environmental Threats**: Climate change, natural disasters, and resource depletion may create concerns about ecological collapse and the potential consequences for human societies.

- **Technological Disruption**: The rapid pace of technological change, coupled with concerns about artificial intelligence, automation, and the future of work, can also fuel feelings of societal instability.

◈ **Social and Cultural Changes**: The rapid shifts in social and cultural norms, sometimes perceived as undermining traditional values, can provoke anxieties about societal breakdown.

Understanding the specific source of the fear allows one to tailor a response that addresses both the emotional and rational aspects of the individual's concerns.

2. Normalize the Fear and Validate Their Feelings

One of the first steps in calming someone who is afraid of societal collapse is to normalize their fear. It's important to recognize that such feelings are not unusual, particularly in the face of significant global challenges. Validating the individual's feelings, rather than dismissing them, helps them feel understood and supported.

For example, you could say:

"It's completely understandable that you feel concerned about the direction of the world right now. Many people are feeling the same way, and it's natural to have fears about the future, especially when so many things seem uncertain."

By offering empathy and understanding, you create an environment where the individual feels safe to express their concerns. Acknowledging their emotions without judgment can help them feel less isolated in their fear, making it easier for them to process their feelings.

3. Offer Perspective: Focus on Historical Resilience

Humans have faced significant challenges throughout history, yet societies have often found ways to adapt, rebuild, and thrive.

Reminding the person that humanity has experienced multiple crises—from wars and plagues to economic depressions and environmental disasters—can help provide perspective on the current situation.

You can point to specific examples in history where societies have overcome immense challenges:

- **World War II**: Despite the catastrophic devastation of the war, which saw millions of lives lost, humanity emerged with a new sense of global cooperation, leading to the formation of the United Nations and various international treaties aimed at preventing further conflict.

- **The Great Depression**: In the 1930s, the United States and much of the world experienced severe economic collapse, yet the eventual recovery was facilitated by programs like the New Deal and the collective effort to rebuild the global economy.

- **The Civil Rights Movement**: In the face of deep racial segregation and systemic inequality, grassroots movements and determined leaders managed to push through transformative social changes that resulted in greater equality for marginalized communities.

These historical examples show that societies are resilient, and even in the darkest times, there are often positive outcomes that arise from collective action and individual perseverance. This sense of historical continuity can help alleviate feelings of doom and encourage hope for the future.

4. Practice Mindfulness

When faced with anxiety about societal collapse, it is easy for the mind to race and become overwhelmed by worst-case scenarios. Mindfulness and grounding techniques can help bring the individual's attention back to the present moment, alleviating some of the panic or distress caused by these fearful thoughts.

Some effective techniques include deep breathing exercises, grounding techniques and meditation.

Deep breathing is a simple and effective way to activate the body's relaxation response. Encouraging slow, deep breaths can help calm the nervous system and reduce feelings of panic.

Grounding exercises can help calm the individual's mind, returning their focus to the present moment and reducing the emotional intensity of their fear.

Meditation involves increasing awareness of bodily sensations and encouraging a calm and relaxed state to interrupt cycles of worry and fear.

5. Encourage Constructive Action and Agency

A significant part of the fear surrounding societal collapse is the sense of helplessness that comes with it. Feeling as though the individual has no control over the outcome can exacerbate anxiety. Encouraging constructive action can help alleviate these feelings of powerlessness and foster a sense of agency.

Suggesting small, actionable steps can make the individual feel more empowered and capable of contributing positively to society, even in times of uncertainty. These actions can range from practical tasks to social engagement:

- **Volunteer Work**: Encourage them to volunteer with local organizations focused on social justice, environmental sustainability, or community-building efforts. Volunteering not only provides a sense of purpose but also creates connections with others who share similar concerns, helping to counter feelings of isolation.

◈ **Political Engagement**: For those concerned about political instability, getting involved in local politics or supporting causes they care about can offer a way to influence change. Participating in town hall meetings, writing to elected officials, or supporting grassroots movements can empower individuals to feel as though they are contributing to a more stable and just society.

◈ **Sustainable Living**: For those worried about environmental collapse, embracing more sustainable practices—such as reducing waste, supporting renewable energy, or planting a garden—can offer a sense of control. Knowing that their actions, no matter how small, contribute to a more sustainable future can ease feelings of dread about environmental decline.

Taking constructive action not only fosters a sense of personal agency but also reinforces the idea that positive change is possible, even in difficult circumstances.

6. Foster Social Connections and Community Building

One of the most important factors in mitigating fear during times of crisis is the presence of strong social connections. Human beings are social creatures, and the support of friends, family, and community can provide both emotional comfort and practical assistance. In times of uncertainty, it is especially important to foster these connections and build a supportive network.

Encourage the individual to reach out to friends or loved ones to discuss their concerns openly. Group therapy, support groups, and online communities that share similar concerns about societal issues can also offer a sense of solidarity and understanding.

Community-building initiatives, such as neighborhood associations, local activism, or even informal gatherings, can help combat isolation and create a sense of shared purpose. Knowing that others are working toward similar goals can provide reassurance and reduce feelings of helplessness.

7. Cultivate Hope Through Optimism and Positive Psychology

A fear of societal collapse often leads individuals to focus on negative outcomes, making it difficult to see the potential for positive change. Cultivating optimism and encouraging a hopeful outlook can provide a much-needed counterbalance to these fears. Positive psychology, which focuses on strengths, resilience, and well-being, offers valuable tools for fostering hope.

Gratitude Practice

Encouraging the individual to practice gratitude can help shift their focus from what's wrong with the world to what's going well. A simple technique is to write down three things each day for which they are grateful. This practice can help build a more positive mindset and remind the individual of the many good things in their life.

Strengths-Based Thinking

Encourage the person to reflect on their personal strengths and resilience. Consider past challenges they have faced and overcome. By highlighting their ability to navigate adversity, they can gain confidence in their capacity to cope with future challenges, no matter how daunting they may seem.

Visualization of Positive Futures

Encourage them to engage in visualization exercises that imagine a positive future—one where societal challenges have been addressed, and the world has found sustainable and peaceful solutions. Visualization can create a sense of hope and motivate individuals to work toward positive outcomes, rather than getting stuck in the fear of collapse.

The fear of societal collapse is a complex and deeply felt anxiety that many people experience in response to a world marked by uncertainty. However, through the combination of psychological techniques, constructive action, social connection, and a focus on hope, individuals can regain a sense of agency, resilience, and calm. By normalizing their fears, providing perspective on historical resilience, engaging in mindfulness practices, fostering optimism, and encouraging social and political engagement, those experiencing fear of societal collapse can begin to navigate their concerns with greater confidence and composure.

Ultimately, reassuring someone who is afraid of societal collapse involves not only calming their immediate anxieties but also offering them a pathway toward active participation, hope, and a deepened sense of connection to the world around them. These techniques allow individuals to confront their fears and reclaim a sense of control in an uncertain world, fostering both personal and collective resilience in the face of societal challenges.

Ways To Take Action

In times of political, social, or economic uncertainty, many Americans experience feelings of fear and anxiety about the future of their country. Concerns about the stability of institutions, the erosion of democratic principles, or the breakdown of social cohesion can feel overwhelming. However, while fear can be paralyzing, it can also act as a powerful motivator for positive change. Fearful Americans can take concrete actions to help stabilize the nation, not only alleviating their own anxiety but also contributing to the strength, unity, and resilience of the country. These actions range from engaging in civic and political activities, to fostering community connections, to advocating for systemic reforms.

This essay will explore a range of actions that fearful Americans can take to promote a more stable and inclusive society. These actions will be divided into several key areas: civic engagement, community involvement, promoting social justice, fostering unity and dialogue, environmental sustainability, and mental and physical well-being.

1. Civic Engagement: Strengthening Democracy Through Action

One of the most powerful ways for fearful Americans to help stabilize their country is through increased civic engagement. A healthy democracy depends on an informed, active electorate that participates in the political process. When citizens feel they have a voice in shaping their nation's future, they are less likely to feel helpless or alienated.

Voting

Voting is the most fundamental and accessible form of civic engagement. In the U.S., elections are the cornerstone of democratic governance, and every citizen has the right and responsibility to vote. Whether in local, state, or federal elections, each vote contributes to the shaping of policy, leadership, and the overall direction of the country.

For Americans who are fearful of political instability, voting offers a direct way to influence change. Fear can often stem from a sense of powerlessness, but voting allows individuals to actively participate in the decision-making process. It is crucial to stay informed about candidates, issues, and voting procedures, and to vote in every election, as even local elections can have significant impacts on the health of democracy.

Advocacy and Activism

Beyond voting, Americans can take action by becoming involved in advocacy and activism. Whether supporting causes such as voting rights, economic justice, healthcare reform, or climate action, advocacy allows individuals to raise their voices and demand action from elected officials. Joining grassroots movements, attending protests, or writing letters to representatives are all ways to influence public policy and hold leaders accountable.

For those who feel fearful of the country's direction, advocating for causes that align with their values can provide a sense of purpose and agency. Many organizations and campaigns are focused on promoting democratic principles, fighting for equality, and protecting human rights. By lending their time, energy, or financial support, fearful Americans can contribute to efforts that work toward a more stable and just society.

Run for Office

For some Americans, the most direct way to contribute to political stability is by running for office. While this may seem like a daunting task, local and state-level offices often serve as entry points for political leadership. By running for office, individuals can directly influence policy and help shape the laws and regulations that govern their communities and the country.

Running for office is a powerful way to take action in the face of fear because it represents a commitment to the democratic process and a belief in the possibility of positive change. Fearful Americans who feel compelled to address issues such as inequality, environmental degradation, or political corruption may find that pursuing a political career allows them to advocate for the reforms they believe are necessary for the country's stability.

2. Community Involvement: Strengthening Social Cohesion

When fear of societal collapse arises, it can often be exacerbated by a sense of isolation or disconnection from others. Building strong, resilient communities is crucial for promoting social cohesion and stability. By getting involved in their local communities, fearful Americans can help create networks of support and solidarity, which can provide both emotional comfort and practical assistance in times of crisis.

Volunteering

Volunteering is one of the most effective ways to foster a sense of community and contribute to positive social change. Whether working at a food bank, helping to clean up local parks, tutoring children, or supporting the elderly, volunteering strengthens the social fabric and provides tangible support to those in need. For individuals who are fearful of societal instability, volunteering can be a powerful way to counteract feelings of helplessness by taking concrete action to improve the lives of others.

Additionally, volunteering connects individuals to others who share similar values and concerns, which can help reduce feelings of isolation. Volunteering can also provide a sense of accomplishment, reinforcing the idea that even small actions can have a meaningful impact on the larger community.

Community Organizing

Community organizing involves mobilizing groups of people around shared goals and interests to address local issues. Whether organizing around issues such as affordable housing, police reform, environmental sustainability, or education, community organizers work to build collective power and effect change at the local level. Fearful Americans can take action by joining or forming community organizations that work toward stabilizing and improving their neighborhoods.

By organizing around common concerns, individuals can create a sense of collective responsibility and action. In times of crisis, communities that are organized and well-connected are better equipped to respond to challenges, support one another, and advocate for necessary reforms.

Fostering Local Economies

Another way to contribute to community stability is by supporting local economies. By buying from local businesses, participating in farmer's markets, and promoting fair trade and sustainable practices, individuals can help ensure that local economies remain strong and resilient. Economic stability at the community level helps provide jobs, supports small businesses, and ensures that people have access to essential goods and services, even in times of national instability.

Supporting local businesses also strengthens social ties, as individuals come to rely on and support their neighbors and fellow citizens. Fearful Americans can take meaningful action by promoting economic resilience in their communities, helping to create a more stable foundation for the future.

3. Promoting Social Justice and Equality

Fear of societal collapse is often linked to concerns about inequality and injustice. A society that is deeply divided, with significant disparities in wealth, opportunity, and access to basic services, is more vulnerable to social unrest and instability. Fearful Americans can take action to help stabilize the country by advocating for social justice and equality, ensuring that all citizens have the opportunity to thrive.

Advocating for Policy Reform

Policy reform is an essential component of addressing systemic issues that contribute to societal instability. Whether advocating for criminal justice reform, healthcare access, affordable education, or labor rights, pushing for policy change can help create a more just and equitable society. Fearful Americans can take action by writing to elected officials, participating in campaigns, and supporting organizations that work to reform policies and institutions that perpetuate inequality.

For those who are concerned about the growing wealth gap, income inequality, or the lack of access to basic human rights, advocating for policies that address these issues can provide a sense of purpose and hope. When people take action to advocate for change, they can influence the direction of national and local policies, contributing to a more stable and fair society.

Supporting Racial and Gender Justice

Racial and gender inequality are central issues that continue to affect the social stability of the United States. Fearful Americans can take action to address these injustices by supporting organizations that advocate for racial and gender justice, participating in protests, and educating themselves and others about these issues. Supporting policies that promote equal rights and opportunities for all people, regardless of race, gender, or background, can help reduce tensions and promote social cohesion.

Participating in or supporting initiatives that address systemic racism, such as the Black Lives Matter movement or gender equity campaigns, can help create a more inclusive society. When people come together to address these issues, they can foster a sense of shared responsibility and create a stronger foundation for societal stability.

4. Fostering Dialogue and Unity

Fear of societal collapse is often fueled by division and polarization. When people feel disconnected from one another, whether due to political differences, cultural conflicts, or ideological divides, the sense of unity that holds society together can begin to fray. Fearful Americans can help stabilize the nation by fostering dialogue and promoting unity, working to bridge divides and cultivate understanding between different communities.

Promoting Cross-Party Dialogue

One of the most significant sources of polarization in American society is political division. Fearful Americans can take action by engaging in cross-party dialogue, participating in conversations with individuals who hold different political views, and finding common ground. While these conversations can be difficult, they can help reduce misunderstandings and foster empathy.

Organizations such as the **Bridge Alliance** and **Living Room Conversations** work to bring people from different political backgrounds together to engage in respectful, productive conversations. By participating in or supporting such initiatives, fearful Americans can contribute to healing political divides and promoting greater unity.

Engaging in Conflict Resolution

In times of social or political unrest, conflicts are inevitable. However, helping to resolve conflicts through nonviolent communication and mediation can prevent tensions from escalating and creating further instability. Fearful Americans can learn and apply conflict resolution skills, helping to foster understanding and cooperation in both their personal lives and their communities.

Conflict resolution techniques—such as active listening, empathy, and finding common ground—can be used to de-escalate situations and create space for meaningful dialogue. These practices can be particularly effective in communities that are divided along political, racial, or cultural lines.

5. Addressing Environmental Sustainability

Many Americans are fearful of the long-term environmental consequences of climate change, deforestation, pollution, and resource depletion. Environmental degradation poses a significant threat to the stability of both local and global communities. Fearful Americans can take action by promoting sustainability and advocating for policies that protect the environment.

Supporting Climate Action

Participating in climate action is one of the most impactful ways to address environmental collapse. Fearful Americans can take part in grassroots movements, support renewable energy initiatives, reduce their carbon footprints, and advocate for stronger environmental protections. By supporting policies that address climate change, such as transitioning to clean energy, reducing waste, and protecting natural habitats, individuals can help safeguard the future of the planet and promote long-term stability.

Promoting Sustainable Agriculture

Supporting sustainable agricultural practices, such as organic farming, regenerative agriculture, and local food systems, can help ensure that food production is both environmentally responsible and economically sustainable. Fearful Americans can support farmers who use these practices and promote policies that encourage sustainable agriculture.

By taking action to protect the environment and ensure that natural resources are used responsibly, individuals can contribute to a more stable and sustainable future.

6. Taking Care of Mental and Physical Well-Being

Finally, individuals who are fearful of societal collapse should take steps to care for their own mental and physical well-being. Anxiety and stress about the future can be debilitating, but by addressing personal well-being, individuals can build the resilience needed to face difficult times and take meaningful action.

Secular Faith

In a world where religious identity and affiliation remain significant in many societies, the idea of "secular faith"—a belief system or set of values rooted in reason, shared human experience, and ethical principles without reliance on religious doctrine—emerges as a concept capable of strengthening a country. Secular faith can encompass diverse forms of commitment to ideals such as justice, equality, human rights, freedom, and environmental stewardship, while remaining outside the boundaries of traditional religious frameworks. This essay explores how secular faith, with its emphasis on collective responsibility, ethical action, and unity based on shared human values, can help strengthen a nation, foster social cohesion, and promote long-term stability.

1. Defining Secular Faith

Secular faith can be defined as a system of belief or commitment grounded in humanistic and rational principles that does not rely on the supernatural or religious doctrines. Instead, secular faith often emphasizes ethical living, personal responsibility, collective well-being, and the improvement of society. In secular faith, the belief in human potential and the betterment of society becomes a guiding force, and individuals draw on secular moral codes (such as those grounded in humanism, secular ethics, or utilitarianism) to shape their decisions and actions.

While secular faith is not necessarily atheistic or agnostic, it stands apart from religious faith in its rejection of divine authority, focusing instead on human agency and collective decision-making. For many, secular faith provides a framework for finding meaning and purpose without relying on religious doctrines or institutions. This form of faith emphasizes a shared vision for the future of society and encourages cooperation between individuals, communities, and governments, regardless of their religious affiliations.

2. Secular Faith as a Unifying Force

One of the key ways secular faith can strengthen a country is by serving as a unifying force that transcends religious and cultural divides. In pluralistic societies, where people come from different backgrounds, faiths, and traditions, secular faith can create common ground by focusing on universal values—such as justice, equality, and human dignity—that are shared by people across faiths and cultures.

Promoting Social Cohesion

Religious diversity can sometimes create divisions within society, as people may identify more strongly with their religious group than with their fellow citizens. These divisions can sometimes fuel conflicts, prejudice, and mistrust, undermining national unity. Secular faith, by contrast, focuses on shared ethical principles rather than religious affiliation, encouraging individuals to work together toward common goals based on mutual respect and cooperation. Secular humanist values, such as the belief in the inherent worth of all individuals and the importance of social justice, can bring people together, regardless of their religious beliefs.

For instance, secular movements advocating for civil rights, gender equality, and freedom of expression often unite people across religious and cultural lines. Secular faith's ability to bring together people of diverse backgrounds helps build social cohesion and foster a sense of national identity rooted in shared ethical commitments rather than religious conformity.

Common Ethical Framework

Secular faith provides a moral and ethical framework that is not bound by religious dogma but is nonetheless rooted in core values such as fairness, empathy, and compassion. For example, secular humanism promotes the idea that humans have the capacity and responsibility to create ethical societies based on reason, justice, and kindness, emphasizing human welfare over adherence to traditional religious teachings. This ethical approach appeals to people of all beliefs and offers a pathway for constructive collaboration toward social progress.

Secular ethics provides guidance in addressing contemporary challenges such as climate change, poverty, inequality, and human rights abuses. It encourages policymakers to act with integrity and empathy, promoting the common good over narrow interests or religious dogma. In this way, secular faith can contribute to the development of ethical, forward-thinking policies that serve all citizens and strengthen the social fabric.

3. Secular Faith and Civic Responsibility

Secular faith can also play a vital role in fostering civic responsibility, a key component of a strong and stable society. As people invest in a vision of society based on shared ethical principles, they are more likely to take responsibility for their communities and their nation's well-being. Civic responsibility is a cornerstone of a functioning democracy and a stable political system, and secular faith encourages individuals to take part in the democratic process, to hold governments accountable, and to work for the betterment of society.

Encouraging Active Citizenship

Active citizenship—being engaged in public life, voting, volunteering, and advocating for positive change—is essential to maintaining a functioning democracy. Secular faith encourages individuals to believe in the importance of their role in society and to view participation in civic life as both a duty and a privilege. Rather than relying on religious institutions or ideologies to dictate behavior, secular citizens are motivated to make decisions based on rational inquiry, evidence-based policies, and concern for the well-being of all.

Secular faith encourages people to be informed and involved in matters such as voting, public discourse, and social activism. Through secular organizations and movements, citizens are empowered to advocate for policy changes that promote justice, equity, and the welfare of society as a whole. As such, secular faith strengthens a nation by ensuring a well-informed, active, and engaged electorate that is dedicated to upholding the principles of democracy.

Building Civic Virtue

Civic virtue—the commitment to promoting the common good, upholding justice, and participating in the welfare of others—is a central tenet of secular faith. Secular humanism, for example, emphasizes the importance of ethics, responsibility, and mutual respect in fostering a just society. These values guide individuals in their everyday actions, encouraging them to act with integrity, empathy, and fairness toward others.

Building civic virtue through secular faith can help mitigate societal challenges such as political polarization, corruption, and apathy. As individuals come to view themselves as stewards of society's well-being, they are more likely to act with consideration for others' needs and work to create a fairer, more just country.

4. Secular Faith and Social Progress

Secular faith also plays an important role in promoting social progress, particularly by championing human rights, equality, and justice. While religious institutions have historically been at the forefront of advocating for moral principles, secular movements have often played a pivotal role in advancing rights and freedoms for marginalized groups, including women, racial minorities, and LGBTQ+ individuals. Secular faith encourages people to critically assess societal norms and question practices that perpetuate discrimination or injustice.

Advocating for Equality

One of the key ways secular faith strengthens a country is by advocating for equality, a foundational principle for social stability. Secular humanism, for example, promotes the idea that all human beings have intrinsic value and deserve equal treatment and opportunities, regardless of their background or identity. Secular faith encourages individuals and governments to confront inequality in all its forms, including racial discrimination, gender-based violence, and economic disparity.

Secular movements have historically led the charge in pushing for civil rights and social justice, from the abolition of slavery to the fight for women's suffrage to the push for marriage equality. By standing up for marginalized groups and advocating for inclusive policies, secular faith helps ensure that everyone has access to the rights and freedoms that are essential for a healthy society.

Fostering Innovation and Reform

Secular faith also encourages the pursuit of knowledge and the use of reason to drive societal progress. As religious traditions are often tied to specific doctrines and beliefs, secular individuals are more likely to challenge outdated practices or beliefs that hinder progress. Secularism promotes scientific inquiry, evidence-based decision-making, and the development of technologies that can improve people's lives and address global challenges.

For example, secular advocacy for scientific research and education has led to important advancements in medicine, technology, and environmental protection. The secular commitment to reason and empirical evidence drives innovation and fosters solutions to pressing societal issues such as climate change, public health, and social inequality. Secular faith encourages individuals to imagine and create a better future based on human knowledge and shared ethical values.

5. Secular Faith and Global Cooperation

In an increasingly interconnected world, nations must work together to address global challenges such as climate change, conflict resolution, and economic inequality. Secular faith, with its emphasis on reason, human dignity, and global responsibility, can promote international cooperation and peace. By fostering a shared understanding of human rights, democracy, and sustainability, secular faith encourages countries to collaborate and work toward the common good.

International Human Rights

Secular faith supports the idea that human rights are universal and should be upheld regardless of cultural or religious differences. Secular movements have been instrumental in advocating for the Universal Declaration of Human Rights, which outlines basic freedoms and protections for all people, regardless of nationality, religion, or background. Secular organizations and governments have been at the forefront of advocating for the rights of refugees, migrants, and oppressed communities, pushing for policies that prioritize the dignity and well-being of all people.

In this way, secular faith fosters global cooperation based on shared values, helping to address the root causes of conflict, inequality, and injustice around the world.

Environmental Stewardship

Secular faith is also aligned with the global movement for environmental sustainability. While religious traditions have varying stances on environmental issues, secular organizations and advocates have been at the forefront of pushing for policies and actions that protect the planet for future generations. Secular humanism, with its focus on reason and evidence, promotes policies that combat climate change, preserve biodiversity, and reduce human impact on the environment.

As countries around the world work together to address environmental crises, secular faith encourages nations to collaborate and take collective responsibility for the well-being of the planet and its inhabitants.

6. Secular Faith and National Resilience

Finally, secular faith strengthens a country by fostering resilience in the face of adversity. While religious faith can provide comfort and support during difficult times, secular faith offers a framework for coping with challenges grounded in human agency and collective action. When individuals and communities face crises such as natural disasters, political upheaval, or economic downturns, secular faith encourages them to come together, collaborate, and rebuild.

Secular faith reinforces the idea that, even in the face of hardship, people have the power to create positive change and build a better future. This sense of empowerment and collective responsibility is key to national resilience and stability, as it motivates citizens to work together toward common goals and navigate challenges with determination and hope.

Secular faith, grounded in reason, ethics, and shared human values, can play a vital role in strengthening a country. By fostering social cohesion, promoting civic responsibility, advocating for social progress, encouraging global cooperation, and building resilience in the face of adversity, secular faith provides a powerful force for positive change. In a world of increasing diversity and complexity, secular faith offers a common ground for individuals to unite and work toward a more just, equitable, and sustainable society. Through these collective efforts, secular faith can contribute to a more stable, prosperous, and harmonious nation, where all people are empowered to reach their full potential and work together for the common good.

Religious Faith

Religious faith has played a significant role in shaping the cultural, social, and political landscape of the United States since its founding. As a nation built on principles of religious freedom and pluralism, America has long been a place where individuals are encouraged to express and practice their faith, whether through organized religion, personal spiritual beliefs, or through community-based initiatives. Religious faith has provided countless Americans with a sense of meaning, purpose, and direction, influencing their actions and decisions in both personal and collective contexts.

This essay explores the many ways in which religious faith can have a positive impact on America. From fostering community engagement and social justice to promoting personal well-being and ethical behavior, religious faith has the potential to contribute significantly to the country's moral and social fabric. By drawing on the diverse traditions, teachings, and practices that define religious life in America, we can explore how faith can serve as a source of strength, hope, and positive transformation in the lives of individuals and the broader society.

1. Religious Faith as a Source of Personal Well-Being

At the core of religious faith is the belief in a higher power, purpose, and a sense of divine guidance. For many Americans, religion serves as a primary source of emotional, psychological, and spiritual well-being. The benefits of religious faith on personal well-being extend beyond mere belief; religious communities and practices also provide individuals with a support system that can help them navigate life's challenges, reduce feelings of isolation, and provide a framework for making ethical decisions.

Psychological and Emotional Support

Religious faith can have a profound impact on mental health and emotional resilience. Many studies have shown that religious individuals tend to report higher levels of life satisfaction and lower levels of depression and anxiety. The practice of prayer, meditation, and reflection on religious texts often provides individuals with moments of peace, solace, and perspective. For people going through difficult times—such as grief, illness, or personal loss—faith can offer comfort and a sense of meaning that helps them cope with adversity.

In times of crisis, religious faith provides a sense of hope and assurance that life has purpose and that challenges are part of a larger divine plan. This emotional and psychological support fosters a sense of optimism and inner peace, helping individuals to remain resilient and hopeful even in the face of hardship.

Guidance in Ethical Decision-Making

Religious faith often provides adherents with a clear moral framework based on the teachings of their respective faith traditions. This framework offers guidance for ethical decision-making, promoting values such as honesty, compassion, integrity, and forgiveness. For individuals navigating complex or morally ambiguous situations, religious teachings can provide clarity and direction, helping them to make choices that align with their faith and principles.

In a society where ethical challenges are ubiquitous, the moral compass provided by religious faith can help individuals make decisions that promote the greater good, contribute to social harmony, and support the well-being of others. By guiding individuals toward virtuous actions, religious faith plays a crucial role in fostering a culture of personal responsibility and accountability.

2. Religious Faith and Community Building

One of the most significant contributions of religious faith to American society is its ability to foster community. Religious institutions, such as churches, synagogues, mosques, and temples, serve as gathering places where people can come together to worship, engage in fellowship, and support one another. In these communities, individuals are not only encouraged to deepen their personal relationship with the divine, but also to form bonds with their neighbors and work together for the common good.

Providing Social Support and Solidarity

Religious communities provide a sense of belonging and connection that can help individuals feel less isolated, especially in times of personal difficulty. Many religious traditions emphasize the importance of mutual support, encouraging members to care for one another, offer emotional and spiritual support, and lend a helping hand in times of need. This communal aspect of faith fosters solidarity and compassion, as religious groups come together to address the needs of their members and the larger community.

For example, religious congregations often provide vital social services, such as food pantries, homeless shelters, mental health counseling, and educational programs. These initiatives not only support individuals within the faith community but also contribute to the well-being of the broader society. By focusing on the needs of others and cultivating a spirit of charity, religious groups help strengthen the social fabric and create a more caring, compassionate nation.

Building Interfaith Understanding

Religious faith in America is diverse, with individuals practicing a wide range of traditions, including Christianity, Islam, Judaism, Hinduism,

Buddhism, and various indigenous faiths. While religious differences may sometimes lead to misunderstandings or tensions, religious communities also have the potential to foster interfaith dialogue and collaboration. By emphasizing common values such as peace, justice, and respect for others, religious faith can help bridge divides between different faith communities, promoting mutual understanding and cooperation.

Interfaith initiatives, such as community service projects, interfaith dialogues, and joint religious observances, help build relationships between people of different faiths. These efforts contribute to a more tolerant and inclusive society, where individuals are encouraged to respect one another's beliefs and work together toward shared goals.

3. Religious Faith and Social Justice

One of the most significant ways that religious faith can positively impact America is by inspiring action toward social justice and equity. Many religious traditions emphasize the importance of caring for the marginalized, fighting for justice, and promoting the dignity and worth of all human beings. Throughout American history, religious faith has been a driving force behind many of the country's most important social movements, from the abolition of slavery to the civil rights movement to contemporary efforts for racial and economic justice.

Advocating for the Poor and Marginalized

Religious faith consistently calls its adherents to care for the poor, the oppressed, and those on the margins of society. The teachings of Jesus, for example, emphasize the importance of helping the least among us, feeding the hungry, sheltering the homeless, and visiting the sick. In the Hebrew Bible, the prophet Isaiah calls for justice for the oppressed and the downtrodden. In Islam, the concept of zakat (almsgiving) calls for individuals to give to those in need, ensuring that wealth is redistributed and that no one is left behind.

Religious groups and leaders have been at the forefront of advocating for policies that address economic inequality, improve access to healthcare and education, and protect the rights of marginalized communities. From supporting the passage of civil rights legislation to participating in protests for fair wages and workers' rights, religious faith has long inspired Americans to work toward a more just and equitable society.

Promoting Peace and Nonviolence

Religious faith also plays a critical role in promoting peace and nonviolence. Many religious traditions teach that individuals should love their enemies, seek reconciliation, and work to resolve conflicts peacefully. The nonviolent principles espoused by figures such as Mahatma Gandhi and Dr. Martin Luther King Jr. were deeply influenced by their religious faith and have had a lasting impact on social movements in the United States.

By promoting the values of peace, forgiveness, and reconciliation, religious faith helps to counteract the forces of hatred, division, and violence that threaten societal stability. Religious leaders and communities continue to advocate for diplomatic solutions to conflicts, the peaceful resolution of disputes, and the building of bridges between people of different backgrounds and beliefs.

4. Religious Faith and National Morality

Religious faith also plays an important role in shaping the moral compass of a nation. In the United States, religious teachings have long influenced the nation's values, particularly in regard to issues such as individual liberty, justice, the rule of law, and the sanctity of life.

Religious faith serves as a foundation for ethical decision-making at both the individual and national level.

Upholding the Rule of Law

Religious faith supports the idea of justice and fairness, encouraging individuals and institutions to act in accordance with the law and to respect the rights and freedoms of others. The concept of justice, which is central to many religious traditions, encourages individuals to stand up for what is right and to seek equitable outcomes in both personal and societal matters.

Religious communities also provide a moral framework for understanding the importance of civic duty and participation in the democratic process. By encouraging individuals to be active in their communities, to vote, and to advocate for policies that promote justice, religious faith helps ensure that the rule of law is upheld and that the country remains a just and moral society.

Instilling Values of Compassion and Kindness

Many religious teachings emphasize the importance of compassion, kindness, and love toward others. The Golden Rule, found in numerous religious traditions, teaches that individuals should treat others as they would like to be treated. This principle of empathy and mutual respect serves as a powerful moral guide for behavior, both on a personal level and in interactions with others.

By promoting values of compassion and kindness, religious faith helps to create a more harmonious society, where individuals are encouraged to care for one another, offer help in times of need, and show understanding toward those who are different from themselves. These values contribute to a positive and inclusive national culture, fostering cooperation, unity, and respect for others.

5. Religious Faith and National Unity

Religious faith can also contribute to national unity by providing a sense of shared identity, purpose, and common values. In a country as diverse as the United States, where people come from various cultural, ethnic, and religious backgrounds, religion can serve as a unifying force that transcends divisions and fosters a sense of belonging.

Creating Shared Moral and Ethical Frameworks

Religious faith provides a shared framework for moral and ethical values that can unite citizens across diverse backgrounds. Many of the foundational principles of American democracy, such as liberty, equality, and the pursuit of happiness, are rooted in religious ideals. By drawing on these common values, religious faith can help Americans find common ground, despite their differences, and work toward the common good.

Fostering National Pride and Patriotism

Religious faith can also inspire a sense of national pride and patriotism. Many Americans view their country as a place where they can live out their religious beliefs freely, and religious faith can help individuals develop a deep love and commitment to the country. This sense of shared identity and purpose fosters a stronger sense of community and solidarity, both within religious groups and across the broader national landscape.

Religious faith has the potential to make a profound and positive impact on America, strengthening the social, cultural, and moral fabric of the nation. From fostering personal well-being and ethical decision-making to promoting community building, social justice, and national unity, religious faith provides a foundation for positive transformation in both individual lives and the broader society. By drawing on the teachings and principles of various religious traditions, Americans can work together to create a more just, compassionate, and resilient nation—one that values human dignity, justice, peace, and the well-being of all its citizens.

Gratitude

Throughout history, there have been countless individuals whose work has transformed society, improved lives, and advanced the ideals of justice, equality, and peace. These individuals, often working behind the scenes or under immense pressure, dedicate their time, energy, and resources toward creating a better world. They are the changemakers who stand up for the marginalized, challenge systems of oppression, and work tirelessly to address social issues that impact the lives of many. Whether they are activists, community organizers, educators, politicians, or everyday citizens who recognize a problem and work toward a solution, the people who actively attempt to affect positive social change deserve profound gratitude.

This essay expresses appreciation for those who, through their words and actions, strive to create a more just, equitable, and compassionate society. By acknowledging their efforts and honoring their contributions, we can celebrate the powerful impact they have on both individual lives and the collective well-being of humanity. The following sections outline various ways in which these changemakers help build a better world and why their efforts merit deep and lasting gratitude.

1. Gratitude for Challenging Injustice and Inequality

One of the most profound ways people contribute to positive social change is by confronting injustice and inequality. Throughout history, people have fought against oppression based on race, gender, sexuality, religion, and class. From the Civil Rights Movement in the United States to the fight for women's suffrage, from the LGBTQ+ rights movement to global campaigns against human trafficking, there are countless examples of individuals who have stood up to challenge systems of inequality and make the world a better place for everyone.

The Courage to Speak Out

Challenging societal injustice requires incredible courage. It often means standing against the status quo, even when that status quo is deeply entrenched and widely accepted. For those who fight for racial justice, for example, it may involve standing up to prejudices that have existed for centuries, and confronting both overt and covert forms of racism. For advocates of gender equality, it might mean fighting against ingrained patriarchal systems and speaking out in the face of discrimination.

Many of these individuals face significant risks—personal, professional, and even physical—to advocate for marginalized communities and ensure that their voices are heard. Yet, they persist because they believe in the fundamental rights of all people and the potential for societal progress. The work of leaders like Martin Luther King Jr., Malala Yousafzai, and Nelson Mandela—who risked their lives for equality—remains an inspiration to all who seek to challenge injustice.

Their efforts have made a tangible difference. The Civil Rights Act of 1964, the rise of the #MeToo movement, and ongoing global efforts to combat human trafficking and modern-day slavery are just a few examples of the lasting impact that those who challenge inequality have had. Their work continues to inspire future generations to take action and demand fairness for all.

Honoring the Unseen Heroes

While many social movements have iconic leaders, it is crucial to remember the countless unsung heroes who also play a pivotal role in fighting injustice. These individuals may not have large platforms or widespread recognition, but they are nonetheless essential in pushing society toward progress. Whether they are community organizers, teachers, grassroots activists, or volunteers, these people dedicate their lives to fighting for the voiceless and ensuring that all individuals have an opportunity to live free from discrimination and prejudice.

Their tireless advocacy and advocacy in local communities create ripple effects that reach far beyond what they can see or comprehend. They fight because they know that lasting change begins with small, local efforts that slowly chip away at the barriers to equality and justice. Their contributions are no less important than the public figures who lead major movements, and they deserve to be recognized and celebrated for their resilience and determination.

2. Gratitude for Promoting Environmental Sustainability

The fight for environmental justice and sustainability is one of the most pressing issues of our time. Climate change, pollution, and the degradation of natural resources threaten not only the survival of the planet but the well-being of future generations. People who actively work to protect the environment and advocate for policies that promote sustainability and conservation play a critical role in ensuring that our planet remains habitable and capable of supporting life.

The Impact of Environmental Activists

Environmental activists work tirelessly to raise awareness about the dangers of climate change, deforestation, and environmental pollution. They speak out against the exploitation of natural resources, demand accountability from corporations, and advocate for stronger laws to protect the environment. From grassroots movements to large-scale global campaigns, these changemakers are crucial in bringing attention to the urgent need for environmental protection.

Leaders like Greta Thunberg, who began by striking from school to demand climate action, have catalyzed a global movement and inspired millions of young people to become involved in environmental activism. Their voices amplify the call for sustainable practices and challenge political and corporate leaders to prioritize the health of the planet over short-term profits.

Everyday Acts of Environmental Stewardship

While high-profile environmental activists receive much attention, everyday individuals and communities also play a significant role in promoting sustainability. Whether through reducing waste, supporting local agriculture, or advocating for renewable energy sources, millions of individuals are working behind the scenes to make a positive impact on the environment. These acts, though often small in scope, collectively have a profound effect on the health of the planet and the future of generations to come.

Local environmental groups and individuals who engage in community clean-up efforts, tree planting, and advocacy for sustainable urban development demonstrate how each person has the power to contribute to a more sustainable future. Their work highlights that environmental change is not solely the responsibility of governments and corporations but is a collective effort that requires the involvement of every individual.

Appreciating Those Who Fight for Future Generations

People who work to protect the environment are acting not just for the present but for future generations. They recognize that the world we leave behind will impact the lives of children, grandchildren, and beyond. These changemakers embody a sense of intergenerational responsibility, and their actions demonstrate a commitment to leaving the world better than they found it. Their work gives us hope for a future in which sustainability is at the forefront of global priorities, and their efforts deserve our deepest gratitude.

3. Gratitude for Advancing Health and Education

The advancement of health and education is another vital area where individuals and organizations contribute to positive social change. From advocating for universal access to healthcare to fighting for equitable education, these changemakers seek to improve the lives of individuals and communities by ensuring that everyone has the opportunity to live healthy, fulfilling lives.

Improving Public Health

Public health advocates and medical professionals work tirelessly to ensure that healthcare is accessible, affordable, and effective. They fight for the right to healthcare for all, regardless of socio-economic status, and strive to reduce health disparities in underserved communities. Public health campaigns to combat diseases such as HIV/AIDS, tuberculosis, and malaria have saved countless lives and significantly improved global health outcomes.

During the COVID-19 pandemic, frontline healthcare workers became the face of bravery and selflessness. Despite the risk to their own lives, doctors, nurses, and healthcare staff worked around the clock to care for the sick and provide comfort to those affected by the virus. Their dedication to preserving life in the face of overwhelming challenges deserves immense gratitude.

Fighting for Educational Equity

Education is one of the most powerful tools for social change. Advocates for educational equity fight for access to quality education for all children, regardless of race, ethnicity, or income level. They work to reduce the achievement gap, improve educational standards, and provide resources to schools that serve low-income communities.

Organizations like Teach for America and various non-profits focused on educational reform are doing the critical work of addressing the systemic issues that perpetuate inequality in education. By pushing for policies that ensure fair funding for schools, advocating for better teacher pay and resources, and promoting curricula that reflect diverse perspectives, these individuals and organizations are creating a more just and equitable educational system.

Their efforts are essential in breaking the cycle of poverty and ensuring that all children have the opportunity to succeed. For every student who graduates, empowered by the knowledge and skills to contribute to society, there is a changemaker working behind the scenes to make it possible.

4. Gratitude for Promoting Peace and Diplomacy

In an increasingly polarized and conflict-ridden world, those who advocate for peace, diplomacy, and nonviolent conflict resolution play a crucial role in maintaining stability and harmony. Whether through international diplomacy, conflict resolution, or grassroots peacebuilding efforts, these individuals and organizations are working to ensure that disputes are resolved through dialogue rather than violence.

Diplomacy and Global Cooperation

Global leaders and diplomats who prioritize peace and cooperation help to resolve conflicts and prevent the outbreak of war. Their efforts in negotiating treaties, mediating disputes, and fostering international relationships can have far-reaching consequences for global stability. The work of the United Nations, as well as peace advocates and organizations working in conflict zones, are examples of how diplomacy and peacebuilding efforts can change the course of history.

Through their commitment to dialogue and understanding, these changemakers contribute to a more peaceful world and prevent the escalation of conflicts that threaten both lives and livelihoods.

Promoting Social Harmony and Reconciliation

Peacebuilders working within countries are equally vital in promoting social harmony and reconciliation, especially in post-conflict societies. Their work focuses on bridging divides, healing wounds, and fostering understanding among different groups. By creating spaces for dialogue and healing, these individuals help to break the cycles of violence and hatred that have torn communities apart.

Their efforts not only restore peace to individuals but also contribute to the long-term stability of societies. Social harmony, fostered through mutual respect and understanding, helps to build a foundation for a peaceful, prosperous future for all.

5. Gratitude for Everyday Acts of Kindness and Civic Engagement

While large-scale movements and efforts to change the world are often celebrated, it is essential to recognize the value of everyday acts of kindness and civic engagement. The person who helps a neighbor, the teacher who stays late to help a struggling student, the volunteer who spends their weekend at a food bank—these individuals may not always be in the spotlight, but their contributions are just as significant.

Contributing to a Culture of Empathy and Compassion

By fostering a culture of empathy and compassion, everyday acts of kindness help create a more harmonious society. People who engage in acts of service and community involvement demonstrate that positive change does not always require grand gestures; sometimes, it is the small, consistent actions that accumulate and create meaningful impact.

Every donation to a charity, every hour volunteered, and every act of kindness helps to strengthen the fabric of society. These contributions, while often unrecognized, are fundamental to the creation of a just and compassionate world.

In a world that often feels divided and uncertain, it is essential to acknowledge and express gratitude toward the individuals and groups who work tirelessly to make a positive difference. Whether they are challenging injustice, promoting environmental sustainability, improving public health, advocating for education, fostering peace, or simply performing acts of kindness, these changemakers are the foundation of a better world. Through their efforts, they inspire hope, encourage action, and remind us that we all have a role to play in creating a more just, equitable, and compassionate society.

For their dedication, selflessness, and unwavering commitment to the greater good, these individuals deserve our deepest gratitude. Let us honor their work, support their efforts, and continue to stand alongside them as we strive to build a better future for all.

The author would like to express gratitude for the countless leaders whose examples inspired this book and for the technology that made it possible. Some of the information included in this publication contains research using artificial intelligence. Activists, journalists, and leaders in all aspects of society contribute to this technology by participating in our culture.

The effect of one person's actions cannot be underestimated.

www.ingramcontent.com/pod-product-compliance
Lightning Source LLC
LaVergne TN
LVHW052311200926
848481LV00002B/532
9798230394013